"No wonder nobody loved me — I was awful!"

"I was in despair. I needed a whole new me — and I didn't know where to get one. Woolies were right out that week. I thought I might just as well — sob — curl up in a mouldy heap — sniff — and die."

BUT JUST AT THAT VERY DESPERATE MOMENT . . .!

"Imagine my surprise when my Fairy Godmother arrived and said . . .
'Do not despair, poor miserable girl —
I have the answer: just give it a whirl!' "

CONTINUED ON PAGE 94

£1.70

# Blue Jeans CONTENTS

## Picture Stories

## Beauty

## Pop and TV

## Readers' True Experiences

## Photo Stories

## Features

## Fashion

## Short Stories

Printed and Published in Great Britain by D. C. Thomson & Co., Ltd., 185 Fleet Street, London EC4A 2HS © D. C. Thomson & Co., Ltd., 1981.
ISBN 0 85116 208 8

# A DIFFERENT KIND OF DREAM...

YOU WERE FED UP AT THE DISCO, BUT YOU DON'T FANCY GOING FOR A COFFEE EITHER. YOU FEEL COOPED UP INDOORS, BUT YOU DON'T WANT TO GO FOR A WALK . . .

YEAH, THAT'S RIGHT.

WHAT'S THE MATTER WITH YOU THESE DAYS, TRACY? YOU NEVER SEEM TO KNOW WHAT YOU WANT TO DO, OR WHERE YOU WANT TO GO! IS IT MY FAULT?

NO IT'S NOT YOU, JEFF. IT'S ME. I JUST WANT TO GO HOME.

I'd known Jeff since we were kids and we'd gone steady for two years. I knew I was being rotten to him, but I couldn't seem to help myself.

'BYE THEN, TRACY. SEE YOU TOMORROW?

I . . . DUNNO. I'LL PROBABLY RING YOU. 'BYE.

HE'S SO GENTLE AND CARING—BUT ALL HIS KIND WORDS JUST IRRITATE ME THESE DAYS! JEFF AND THIS VILLAGE— THEY MAKE ME FEEL SO TRAPPED!

Then, as I turned the corner to the house . . .

OOOPS, SORRY!

OH! HELLO! WHO ARE YOU?

MY NAME'S SIMON AND I'M YOUR FRIENDLY NEW FARM HAND!

OH, THAT'S RIGHT, I REMEMBER DAD SAID HE WAS TAKING ON EXTRA HELP. I'M TRACY—PLEASED TO MEET YOU.

Simon had travelled all around the world, working wherever he could find a job. He had a nice way with him and I could tell my folks liked him.

COME ON, SIMON, EAT UP! I'M SURE YOU'VE ROOM FOR ANOTHER SCONE.

MM, I HAVEN'T TASTED ANYTHING THIS GOOD SINCE I WAS A KID, MRS KIRK.

FEEL FREE TO WATCH TV WITH US IF YOU LIKE, SIMON.

THANKS, BUT I'M A BIT TIRED. IT MUST BE ALL THAT FRESH COUNTRY AIR! I RECKON I'LL JUST PLAY A COUPLE OF TUNES ON MY GUITAR—THAT ALWAYS SENDS ME TO SLEEP! 'NIGHT, FOLKS!

GOODNIGHT, SIMON . . .

His room was over the old stable opposite mine and I could hear him playing . . .

THE WAY HE SMILED AT ME, THE SOUND OF HIS MUSIC—IT MAKES ME FEEL SAD AND HAPPY AT THE SAME TIME. IT'S AS THOUGH HE'S A SPECIAL PERSON I'VE BEEN WAITING FOR . . . ALL MY LIFE.

And . . .

THANKS FOR YOUR HELP, TRACY. WE'LL BE FINISHED IN HALF THE TIME.

OH, WHEN YOU LIVE ON A FARM YOU GET USED TO TAKING A TURN WITH THE CHORES.

The truth was, I found myself wanting to be near him.

Work over for the day, he said he was going for a stroll, and invited me along . . .

WHEREVER I AM, I LIKE TO EXPLORE THE PLACE PROPERLY, FIND OUT A BIT OF THE HISTORY.

YOU MUST'VE BEEN TO LOTS OF EXCITING PLACES.

He had. And I couldn't hear enough about his travels . . .

GREECE WAS FANTASTIC, TRACY. SO WARM AND FRIENDLY, AND BEAUTIFUL, TOO.

BUT I RECKON THE SCENERY IN NORWAY IMPRESSED ME MOST. IT REALLY TOOK MY BREATH AWAY.

OH, SIMON, IF YOU ONLY KNEW WHAT IT DOES TO ME, HEARING YOU SPEAK OF THE THINGS YOU'VE DONE AND SEEN . . .

I FEEL ALL CHURNED UP INSIDE, SO RESTLESS, LIKE A BIRD TRAPPED IN A CAGE. I JUST LONG TO BREAK OUT AND SEE THE WORLD LIKE YOU.

YES, I KNOW EXACTLY WHAT YOU MEAN. IT WAS THE SAME FOR ME.

He'd lived with an elderly uncle who'd wanted him to go to college when he left school . . .

BUT I'D HAD ENOUGH OF STUDYING AND ROUTINE. I KNEW I HAD TO GET OUT INTO THE WORLD AND START LIVING!

WHEN I LEAVE SCHOOL AT THE END OF THIS TERM, DAD WANTS ME TO START IN HIS FRIEND'S OFFICE.

BUT I'VE LIVED HERE ALL MY LIFE. I—I MUST GET AWAY OR I'LL GO MAD!

A GIRL ON HER OWN CAN'T GO HITCHING AS FREELY AS A GUY. BUT I CAN GIVE YOU A FEW ADDRESSES, IF YOU LIKE—PLACES ABROAD WHERE YOU CAN WORK AND STAY A WHILE.

I'VE BEEN MOVING ON FOR NEARLY THREE YEARS NOW, AND I'VE DISCOVERED THAT IT'S NOT JUST THE TRAVELLING I'M AFTER. I THINK I'M LOOKING FOR SOMETHING—ONLY I'M NOT QUITE SURE WHAT . . .

Simon seemed to have opened a door for me and I was so excited at the thought of leaving home. But, in the meantime, I showed him all the local places of interest . . .

THAT CHURCH OVER THERE— THEY SAY IT WAS BUILT NEARLY A THOUSAND YEARS AGO.

ALL THOSE PEOPLE WHO'VE PASSED THROUGH IT . . . JUST THINK . . .

AND THINK OF ALL THE PRETTY GIRLS WHO'VE BEEN KISSED UNDER THIS ANCIENT OAK TREE!

HE MAKES ME FEEL WONDERFUL, ALL LIT UP AND GLOWING INSIDE...

Poor Jeff was the last person on my mind. And . . .

WHAT'RE YOU PLAYING AT, TRACY? YOU'RE NEVER IN WHEN I PHONE, AND NOW YOU'RE MAKING EXCUSES NOT TO COME OUT WITH ME.

YOU KNOW WE'VE BEEN HAVING EXAMS AT SCHOOL. I'VE BEEN BUSY.

YOU MANAGED TO FIND TIME TO GO OUT WITH YOUR NEW FARM HAND! I'M NOT STUPID, TRACY. I'VE SEEN YOU ROUND THE VILLAGE WITH HIM. IT'S QUITE OBVIOUS YOU'VE FALLEN FOR HIM!

NO, JEFF, YOU'VE GOT IT WRONG! YOU DON'T UNDERSTAND ABOUT SIMON!

YOU'LL JUST GET HURT, Y'KNOW. HE'S A DRIFTER AND THAT SORT NEVER STAY LONG. AND WHEN HE DOES GO, I'LL STILL BE HERE, STILL LOVING YOU.

JEFF, DON'T...PLEASE!

IF SIMON GOES, I'LL LOSE TRACK OF HIM. I MIGHT NEVER SEE HIM AGAIN AND I COULDN'T BEAR THAT.

BUT I'M THE ONE WHO HASN'T UNDERSTOOD WHAT'S BEEN HAPPENING. JEFF'S RIGHT—I HAVE FALLEN FOR SIMON!

Over the weeks he'd been with us, Simon and I had become very close, but he'd never actually said he loved me . . .

TRACY, YOU LOOK SO SAD TONIGHT. WHAT'S WRONG?

I'M SO MIXED UP, SIMON. YOU KNOW THOSE ADDRESSES YOU GAVE ME? WELL—I'VE REALISED THAT I DON'T WANT TO GO THERE. I STILL WANT TO TRAVEL, BUT . . .

. . . OH, SIMON, I WANT TO GO WITH YOU! PLEASE LET ME COME ALONG WITH YOU WHEN YOU LEAVE HERE. I WON'T BE ANY TROUBLE AND . . .

HEY, STEADY ON, LOVE. I'M NOT GOING ANYWHERE.

But, a few days later, as we watched the sunset over the village . . .

Then I explained how my heart had been in turmoil ever since he'd told me he was staying.

So, after I left school that summer, I made arrangements to work in a French vineyard . . .

But I was in tears, as I said goodbye to Simon.

For there were other girls in our village and I knew by trying to find the excitement I wanted, I risked losing the love I wanted just as much . . .

**THE END**

# MAKE A DATE WITH FATE!

You don't need a crystal ball to see into the future, y'know. Take a sneaky peak into tomorrow with our special star chart — it'll reveal what's in store for YOU — fame, fortune and fellas!

## ARIES
### (March 21-April 20)

**LOVE:** You fall for dynamic, flashy fellas as a rule. Will you never learn? They're too much competition because *you* like the limelight, too — right? Look for more down-to-earth, sincere types for a steady relationship.

**CAREER:** Ambitious and adventurous is Miss Aries, so running a travelling disco or organising things for a business tycoon would appeal to you. But don't overstep the mark with bosses at first. You can be too outspoken at times.

**FAME:** Looks possible! Either that, or you'll sit at home dreaming up get-rich-quick schemes. Your trouble is, you get bored easily and give up. Your ideas are great, so stick with them!

**FORTUNE:** Probably! Lots of money will pass through your hands — and down the drain if you're not more cautious. Try to hang on to what you've got, and don't take risks.

## TAURUS
### (April 21-May 20)

**LOVE:** Headstrong, passionate but home-loving — what a combination! Lots of boys are attracted to you, but scared off by your possessiveness. Try to control that jealousy.

**CAREER:** Bright and popular, you love to put your views over to anyone who'll listen — you'd make a good politician. Take time to think over important matters as you're a bit too impulsive at times!

**FAME:** If politics aren't your scene, you could earn praise with your cooking skills. Didn't know you had any? The way you love food, you're bound to be a gifted chef!

**FORTUNE:** Open and honest, you make friends easily. You make money easily, too, but you're much too generous with all those great mates, and the cash just seems to slip through your fingers.

## GEMINI
### (May 21-June 20)

**LOVE:** Frantic, excitable Gemini girls need a stronger partner who can calm them down and keep their feet on the ground. Look for an understanding boy who'll put up with your changeable moods.

**CAREER:** Chatterboxes like you would do well in TV or radio. So long as you let others get a word in edgeways and listen to what they say sometimes.

**FAME:** Gemini girls are proud and love praise, so you probably *know* you'll be a star some day! And once you set your mind to something, you usually get it.

**FORTUNE:** If you stopped attempting to try everything at once, and concentrated your abilities on one goal in life, you just *might* end up filthy rich!

## CANCER
### (June 21-July 21)

**LOVE:** Quiet, shy Cancerians can easily be overlooked in a crowd — or even on their own! Build up some confidence and be a bit bolder in future — once boys actually notice you, they'll come flocking.

**CAREER:** You're a home-loving girl at heart, and you adore children and animals. A job as a vet, nanny or nurse would suit you down to the ground.

**FAME:** Sorry! Not a lot of hope here. If you were ever shoved into the spotlight, you'd probably run a mile. But with your loyal, loving nature, you could easily end up as the real power behind a famous fella.

**FORTUNE:** You could be lucky and win the pools! Otherwise, it doesn't look likely you'll ever make the million stakes — you're not pushy or aggressive

and you don't have a lot of business sense. Why worry? You know that the really valuable things in life are love and care. You're already rich.

## LEO
### (July 22-Aug. 21)

**LOVE:** You've got plenty to spare, and you get your fair share, too! But be wary of those brash types you tend to attract; don't be taken in by their sweet-talking and you won't be let down so often.

**CAREER:** You're not fussy — anything will do so long as it keeps you frantically busy! With your endless supply of energy, anything from a disco dancer to a gym teacher would be ideal.

**FAME:** You never know, you might make Legs & Co! Another possibility is to become a sports superstar — but you put fair play above winning so it's unlikely you'd have enough ruthless dedication. Acting is well-starred, though.

**FORTUNE:** No chance! As soon as you could make it, you'd spend it — or give it away. You're extravagant and over-generous. Ah, but you're lovely!

10

# VIRGO

### (Aug. 22-Sept. 21)

**LOVE:** Given half a chance, you'd like to change boys as often as clothes! But deep down you need security. Try not to bottle up those secret emotions — then maybe boys could get through to the *real* you . . .

**CAREER:** You love change and travel; you're quick-witted and clever with languages; you're a superb socialiser and enjoy meeting new people . . . do we really need to tell you what a terrific reporter you'd make? Or perhaps you'd like to be a courier for a travel firm?

**FAME:** Modest Miss Virgo doesn't like shoving herself in front of an audience. Besides, you're scared of criticism, so you'd hate to be always in the public eye. But you could be a friend of the famous.

**FORTUNE:** You're probably artistic, so your work might sell for a fortune — and you're organised enough to hold on to it. But it's more likely you'd want to spend it all on diamonds, furs and the good life!

# LIBRA

### (Sept. 22-Oct. 22)

**LOVE:** A smart girl like you will have a talent for weighing up the good guys and spotting the wolves a mile off. But you're a bit too stand-offish to make mates easily. Don't act so cool!

**CAREER:** Chances are you're not a career girl at heart. You like a comfortable family life most of all. That's OK, but don't rush to settle down too soon.

**FAME:** You'll be a star among your friends, for your sweet and loving nature — but famous? Not unless there's room for another Florence Nightingale!

**FORTUNE:** Your idea of riches is a home that's happy, bright and cheerful, friends who are fun to be with and a family raised on love. Sounds like a good idea, too.

# SCORPIO

### (Oct. 23-Nov. 21)

**LOVE:** Mystery girls make guys go weak at the knees — especially when they're hot stuff, like you! Don't get too secretive, though. It could give the impression you're a two-timer.

**CAREER:** You come into your own at sales time, with your sharp ability to get a good deal. Think about crossing the counter and becoming a seller yourself, or a buyer for a big store.

**FAME:** You're not particularly interested in bright lights and glamour, so you won't chase stardom. Of course, if it came to you, you wouldn't say no.

**FORTUNE:** You're a giving person — not a taker, so it's doubtful you'd ever build up a big bank balance. In fact, if you don't become a bit more selfish, you'll end up broke!

# SAGITTARIUS

### (Nov. 22-Dec. 20)

**LOVE:** Innocent and sweet-natured, you can't fool anyone by hiding your feelings. Any boy you fall for will know all about it! Pick a nice guy who won't walk all over you.

**CAREER:** Dreams of being rich, famous and loved by the whole world are fine — but they *are* just dreams. You'd be better off applying some hard work to take you to the top.

**FAME:** Being a frantic socialiser, your parties will be the toast of the town. You're the hostess with the mostest — but you could find it tricky, trying to top your success with each party having to be even better than the last one.

**FORTUNE:** Be more cautious with cash. You're far too extravagant. Remember you can still enjoy yourself for next to nothing; if you have *real* friends, you can have fun for free.

# CAPRICORN

### (Dec. 21-Jan 19)

**LOVE:** Your independent nature attracts plenty of boys, but it also threatens most of them! Play down the self-sufficient streak before you really do end up fending for yourself.

**CAREER:** Determined but domineering,

that's you. Chances are you'll rise to the top in any job, but you may make a lot of enemies on the way. Don't tread on too many toes.

**FAME:** That overpowering personality will probably shoot you into the public eye — but you may be more notorious than famous. You'll have to choose between fame and friendship if you're truly ambitious.

**FORTUNE:** It's more than likely, as you can be a bit of a Scrooge at times. Ah well, at least you make every penny count. You'll never be totally broke.

# AQUARIUS

### (Jan. 20-Feb. 18)

**LOVE:** Fellas are queueing up for your sort! But make sure you stick to the footloose, fancy-free and fun-loving ones, at least till you know where you're heading in life.

**CAREER:** Dreamy by nature, you could become dozy if you don't apply yourself. Although you hate work, you can't build security on daydreams — unless you become an inventor. That's your best chance of sure-fire success, job-wise.

**FAME:** Being unconventional, your way-out ideas and actions could get your pic in the papers! But you'd probably want to retire from the scene then, because you don't really like publicity.

**FORTUNE:** You're a one-off, and if you put your individual ideas into practice, you could strike gold. Just watch you're not too way-out, and *never* gamble.

# PISCES

### (Feb. 19-March 20)

**LOVE:** Uh-oh, here comes trouble! Any boy who talks big can have you under his thumb in minutes. Big-shots are your downfall — they take advantage of your easy-going nature. And you never learn.

**CAREER:** Such creativity! You'd make a good artist, writer or even cook, but you like your home comforts far too much to give them up in the quest for a hotshot career.

**FAME:** So you were born without confidence . . . but why can't you build some? Your shyness attracts you to fame — but only on the fringes. You couldn't handle it yourself.

**FORTUNE:** Talented you certainly are, but you're a big softie with it. Even if you made a mint in life, you'd soon find some deserving souls to share it with. Try to be a bit tougher, and you could spot a few fakes who are only out to take advantage of your good nature.

# I'D NEVER NEEDED TO CRY

## A READER'S TRUE EXPERIENCE

# I was always the one who had to listen to the heartbreak stories, and Lucy's sounded just like all the rest . . .

**M**R HENDRICKS was always on at me to stay at school and try to get into art college eventually. "Don't you realise," he used to say to me, "what you'll be giving up if you leave school? Your work's not just good, Susan, it's outstanding!" He used to embarrass me by saying that.

I love art. I've always loved it since I was a kid. I could sit for hours, just looking at the changing shapes and colours of clouds, watching leaves tremble, and turn to different shades of green in tumbling winds, studying a slow sunset. Colour and light excite me. But I'd never thought of them as part of my future.

My future had been all planned out for me and by me since I was thirteen.

That's when Dave and I first started realising that our childhood friendship was steadying into something that could last for ever.

Yes, I know that thirteen's early to decide on the rest of your life. But when, like Dave and I, you've always lived in the same street, always spent all your free time together, always laughed at the same jokes and danced to the same music, it's just one of those inevitable things.

Mum understood. She'd been married at sixteen herself, and she and Dad had never had any problems. And they were best friends with Dave's parents.

"Just save up enough money for a deposit on a house," she told us, when she realised how serious we were, "and then you can get married."

I was fifteen by that time, and Dave was eighteen, just coming to the end of his apprenticeship. He'd done well, coming out top of his group at the day release classes, and all set for a good job as an electrician. We were comfortable together, Dave and I, settled and happy in each other's company. Some of the girls at school used to ask, "How can you stand him after all that time?" but when I started explaining about the easy feeling of knowing that he was always there, always warm, always loving and reliable, I could see that they didn't understand.

They were all up one minute and down the next, frantic with happiness or clogged up with despair because someone had smiled at them, or hadn't smiled at them, or smiled at someone else.

"You're far too steady, Susan!" Cath used to complain.

That's the way I was, I suppose. I liked everything to be smooth and unhurried, pleasantly settled and gentle. I suppose that's why I'd always loved Dave's quiet ways, his shy humour, the way he never argued or moaned. He'd just grin at me when I got upset about something, and let the softness of his blue eyes lull me into steadiness again.

## ESCAPE

I just wished Mr Hendricks would stop getting at me all the time. You see, I never thought of my love for art as part of the way I really am. It got in my way, all the turbulence and emotion of painting, almost as if something very deep inside me cried to escape, and disturbed my concentration on things that really mattered.

When I sat down to paint or draw, that something took over, stirring me up with terrible frantic energy and concentrated power. I didn't like the feeling at all.

"It's a gift. You mustn't waste it!" he'd tell me.

But to me it wasn't a case of wasting it, but holding it down, keeping it in its place. I was going to leave school, find an office job, add to the savings in the building society and look forward to the day when Dave and I could get married, and live in our own house, the way we'd planned to do.

By the time I was eighteen I'd have everything I'd ever dreamed about, and the beautiful white wedding that Dad had promised me.

Just to keep Mr Hendricks quiet, though, I went to the art classes at the polytechnic in town twice a week. He thought I ought to do some life drawing, and some pottery, as well as the O-level work I was doing in school.

I didn't really mind going to the classes, because Dave was still going to a couple of evening courses, too, and although we didn't have classes on the same nights, we used to grumble together about the polytechnic coffee bar, and Mr Tompkins, the mean-faced security officer, and the fact that the college was always too cold in the winter, and too hot in the summer.

And we'd chat about our own classes, and sometimes I'd show Dave one of the drawings I'd done, and he'd smile and say I was improving and perhaps I'd be able to paint walls and woodwork in our house if I went on practising.

Witty fellow.

I made a few friends at the classes, too. Most of them I'd just nod to, but some, like Maggie and Sandra and Lucy, I'd meet in the mid-evening break and we'd chatter and giggle about our courses. They were all on a secretarial course, and they'd all left school. I used to ask them about the work they did, and Maggie said she'd let me know if there were any vacancies coming up that summer for girls who could type and doodle in the margins at the same time!

## PROBLEMS

Then, one Thursday evening, Lucy didn't turn up at our usual table.

"She's a bit upset," Maggie told me. "Boy trouble — you know!"

We'd never talked about boyfriends, or anything like that. We never really had time, but that evening, Maggie and Sandra were deep into sorting out Lucy's problems and what she ought to do about it all.

"She's crazy. She hasn't known this guy for more than a couple of weeks and he's turned her into a nervous wreck already!" Sandra said. "I've never seen her like this. He must be something special."

"From what I've heard," Maggie whispered confidentially across the table, "there're a few problems. He's supposed to be going out with someone else . . ."

I switched off. I'd heard it all before at school. Falling in love, for some girls, was just a matter of making mistake after mistake, going head over heels for some boy who strung them along, and made excuses, and two-timed them. I was glad I'd never had to face the heartbreak of being in love with someone who was just using me.

I zipped away to the cloakroom to wash my paint-stained hands and count my lucky stars.

But on the way past the students' TV lounge, I heard someone crying as if the world had come to an end, and there was Lucy, sitting on one of the settees, sobbing her heart out.

## SMUG

I liked Lucy. She had a wicked sense of humour and twinkly green eyes, and a way of saying things right out loud that you've always thought about, secretly, but never dared to say to anyone. She was the one with all the jokes that kept us giggling through the coffee breaks.

"Hey!" I murmured. "What's up? It's not like you!"

I squeezed on to the settee next to her and offered her a clean tissue from my bag. Suddenly, as she broke into another fit of desperate sobbing, and rested her head on my shoulder. I felt like someone's mother.

"Weren't you ever young?" Cath sometimes groaned at me. I somehow knew what she meant. The calm certainty I carried around with me belonged to someone who should have been a lot older than fifteen.

I wondered if I looked smug and self-satisfied to other people, people like Lucy, howling on my shoulder, and at least two years older than me. I'd never needed to cry like that, not once.

"Oh, Susan," she sniffed. "It's a mess, isn't it?"

"What is?" I asked.

"Loving someone. It's always such a mess. I sometimes wonder who those

**Continued on page 16** **13**

# A First Time For Everything...

*The first love of your life isn't likely to be the last, but your first kiss is the one you'll remember always!*

## First Meeting

THE day you wake up feeling great and decide to dress yourself up so's you look great too, *isn't* the day you're likely to meet your love of the year!

When we asked around, most girls seem to have met their guys in strictly non-storybook surroundings. Like when they've been covered in grease helping big bruvver mend his motorbike, or when they've just been to the dentist and their face is half frozen, or when they're red with sunburn and their hair's full of sand, or just when they're not really at their best.

If you only get dressed up when you're on the lookout for a dream boy you could give the appearance that you're on a manhunt!

The ideal solution is to look your best *all* the time. Not easy, we know, but if you get into a healthy, clean-living routine you should feel and look good *most* of the time. And, when you *do* go out looking for romance, try to dress fairly casually rather than plastering yourself with make-up and wearing your newest clothes. Boys, generally, like to feel they chose you, not that you tracked them down!

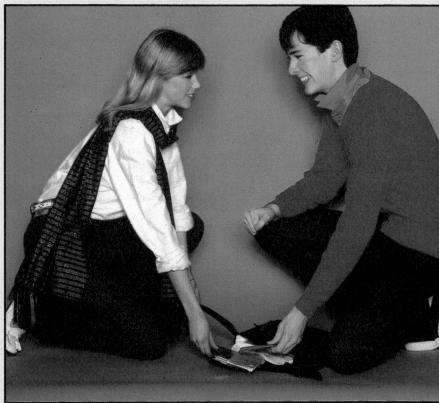

## First Date

The first time he asks you out, don't expect a big deal.

He may want you to stand in a windy field for two hours, watching him play football. Or he may take you for coffee and sit there for an hour saying nothing more than, "Good coffee, isn't it?"

Don't panic! He's not a moron — he's probably just shy. He may also be short of cash, and unable to afford anything more romantic.

If he's not a great talker you can't sit silently all evening, so get him to talk by asking him about his interests. If you don't know what they are you'll have to ask, which is a start. Don't just say, "What are your interests?" Try, "Did you see 'Top Of The Pops' this week?" or "What's your favourite sport?"

If you like him, even if it wasn't the greatest evening in the world, thank him for a nice time when you part. If he's hopeless, but wants to see you again, drop him gently.

"Sorry, we're going to my auntie's next Saturday, but I expect I'll see you around."

# First Love

Although you'll like the first boy you go out with and enjoy his company and like kissing him, you probably won't fall in love with him. That's something special that doesn't happen every time.

How do you know when you're in love? Well, it's not like having the measles — there's no specific set of symptoms that you can tick off and say, "Yes, got that, got that — I must be in love!"

It's a feeling that tends to creep up on you. You catch sight of him unexpectedly, or he does something unusual, and your heart skips a beat. You know you never want anything to hurt this special person.

When you find yourself doing things to please him — not out of terror that he'll leave you, but because you want him to be happy; when you talk about him all the time — not to show off to your friends, but because he's always in your thoughts; when you want to be with him always — not so you can be sure he's not seeing someone else, but because you're happiest in his company — you're in love.

Should you tell him? It'll be hard not to. And if he's said he loves you, then go ahead. But if he hasn't, don't try to bully him into it by announcing your feelings at every opportunity. Murmur it when he kisses you, show it in the way you treat him . . . and let that wonderful "I'm-always-happy-when-I'm-with-her" feeling creep up on him in its own good time.

Don't try to force him to say he loves you or you'll just scare him off. He'll say it when he's good and ready!

# First Quarrel

Mothers and fathers quarrel. Brothers and sisters quarrel. *People* quarrel — so it isn't surprising that you and your boyfriend sometimes quarrel. It's often a silly, small thing that starts it off. You comment that he's wearing his jeans again, he accuses you of not liking his jeans, you say they *are* boring, he says you think *you're* always so smart . . . and soon the neighbours are fitting double glazing to keep out the noise!

But however small the spark that started it, a quarrel is a sign that one of you isn't happy. Maybe you feel that he gets his way all the time, or isn't being as loving as he might be.

A quarrel can clear the air — bring out the hurt feelings and put right the problems causing them.

A quarrel can be mended — when you both try to put it right.

A quarrel can be a new beginning — a stronger, more trusting relationship.

Or a quarrel can be the end . . .

# First Broken Heart

You love him — he knows you do — but he's left you. And now you know why it's called a broken heart, because part of you really does feel broken.

You'll want to cry and cry — go ahead. You'll want to pour it all out to anyone who'll listen — so talk. You've been hurt, and you need time to feel better.

Don't hang around him hoping he'll change his mind. Don't send friends round with messages of love or hate.

It'll be hard, but try to face the fact that people grow at different rates. You aren't a failure — he just grew away from you.

And think, too, how different you are now from that shy little girl he first met. Because your first experience of love will have changed you as a person — and made you ready for your second . . . and maybe *this* love will be for ever.

# First Kiss

Good or bad, you'll remember your first kiss all your life — because it's the one you'll judge all the others against. Don't expect it to be like a film kiss, where a couple look deeply into each other's eyes then move slowly together until their mouths meet in a magnetic kiss. They can do it because they've rehearsed it twenty-four times. You may not find it so easy to land on target, but don't worry — you'll get better with practice!

And if he's moving towards you with a soft look in his eyes, and you think this is it — smile gently, but keep your lips almost closed. Inexperienced kissers often do painful things to each other's teeth! When your lips touch, put your arms round him, close your eyes and enjoy it. Remember to breathe through your nose — don't just hold your breath and go blue in the face!

There! Easy, isn't it? But perhaps you'd better have another go, to be sure you got it right . . .

lucky people are who end up with the right person. I'm surprised anyone manages to stay sane that long!'' She smiled through her tears.

## SMILE

I smiled, too. I didn't tell her that I was one of those lucky people who'd ended up with the right person. I'd never mentioned Dave.

"Yeah!" I said.

"We really go through it, don't we? I mean, look at me! I'm absolutely crazy over this guy, head over heels in love, and it's doing me no good at all. He just has to look at me and I collapse into a heap, and I can't stop thinking about his smile. It's one of those long, slow smiles, know what I mean?" she sighed.

I did. Dave had a smile just like that, a long, slow, comforting smile.

"I know!" I sighed, too.

"It burns you up, doesn't it? The tingle starts in my back and works right through to my fingertips, until I'm on fire all over. Ooooh!" She shuddered. "I wish he wouldn't look at me like that!"

I realised we weren't talking about the same thing. Dave had never turned on a smile that set me on fire. He'd never turned me upside down and inside out. He just smiled, and everything was all right.

"And, you know, Sue," she gasped, "I don't think I can live without it all! It's terrible, and it hurts, and if I can't see him again I just don't want to go on. I know this feeling's not wrong, and he says it's exactly the same for him, a sort of desperate aching feeling, but . . . he's got someone else!"

She collapsed again into helpless tears and sobbing. She sounded desperate. I'd never felt that ache, but I could see how much it was hurting, and I wondered why I'd never been so hopelessly moved and churned up by the love I shared with Dave.

Yet, perhaps the feeling was in me, too, deep down. Sometimes, just sometimes, when I was painting, I felt helpless like that, burned up with feelings, almost scared by them, frighteningly alive, the way I never felt with Dave.

"I'm sorry, Lucy," I murmured.

"D'you think I ought to see him again, on Tuesday, after classes? He says I'm

# I'D NEVER NEEDED TO CRY

Continued from page 13

**We were comfortable together, Dave and I, settled and happy in each other's company . . .**

tearing him in two, but . . . He's fantastic! He's sort of tall and blond and . . . fiery! Sounds daft, doesn't it? But it's as if sparks seem to fly between us and . . . he's the most exciting guy I've ever met! His name's Dave. He's on the Electrical Engineering course, but he's . . ."

"Only here for another three months," I said, finishing the sentence for her. I felt myself saying the words, but couldn't feel anything else.

All my safe castles in the air had just crumbled around my head. My Dave, my nice, steady Dave, the boy next door, someone who smiled and held my hand and talked sense into me; my nice, steady Dave had fallen in love with someone else.

I'd been certain that the quiet reliability was love. But I'd just listened to Lucy talking about the real

thing, about sparks and fire and tingling and excitement and aching.

I'd heard her talk about a boy I hardly knew at all, though I'd known him all my life.

She'd seen a side of Dave that he'd never shown to me. She'd seen life in him, and despair and need. I'd only seen him as someone to lean on. He loved her. I knew from the way she spoke about him, that he loved her as painfully as she loved him. And he'd said nothing to me.

He'd just been quieter than usual, gentler than usual, looking at me when he thought I wasn't watching. Perhaps he was trying to tell me . . .

## TEARS

"D'you know him?" Lucy gasped. "Hey, d'you really know him? D'you live near him or something? Have

you ever seen this girl he's getting engaged to? I'd like to know what she looks like. He says she's lovely. He says he couldn't hurt her . . . but he doesn't know how much he's hurting me, and himself probably . . ."

Two slow tears trickled down my cheeks.

"Weren't you ever young?" I thought about Cath's words again. I felt young now, a small, hurt and frightened kid facing, for the first time in her life, a growing-up problem. I'd bottled up all the real highs and lows and pretended that I was sailing along smoothly.

Only my painting told me, sometimes, what I was missing. And now Lucy had told me, too. There's more to love than being comfortable. There's more to life than being comfortable.

"His girl?" I murmured, wiping away the tears. "Yeah, she's OK, I suppose. A bit dull. I reckon you'd think she was smug and self-satisfied. But I think you're right. He ought to tell her. He's hurting himself if he doesn't!"

"I knew *you'd* understand!" Lucy sighed. "Doesn't it help to talk to someone? Hey, look at the time. I'm late for the second half! Do I look OK? Thanks, Sue! I'm going to see him on Tuesday. You've talked me into it!" She gave me a wobbly smile, rubbed at her eyes with the tissue, gave me a quick hug, and raced out.

I sat in the emptiness and the silence, wondering what I was going to do with the rest of my life after I'd told Dave that he was free. That night was the first time I really cried. It was the night I woke up from a dream I'd lived in for fifteen years.

And I don't regret it all. I don't regret the loneliness and the black despair, the tears howled into every dark empty night, the sickening ache of watching Dave running down the street towards his new girl. Because all that's a long time ago now, and I've cried over a few other boys since, and I've laughed a lot, too.

I've learned what it's like to be young and alive and to battle with all the emotions that I'd hidden inside me. I've started to grow up. And I'm really looking forward to starting at art college next year, next summer.

Who knows what's going to happen then? Perhaps that spark'll fly that Lucy told me about, eighteen months ago.

*Would she ever let me close enough to find out . . .*

# The Colour Of Her EYES

TWENTY MINUTES LATE, ON THE MOST IMPORTANT DAY OF MY LIFE! THAT TRAIN JUST HAS TO TURN UP! CHRISTINE MIGHTN'T WAIT MUCH LONGER! SHE'S SO SCARED AND UNSURE OF HERSELF, EVEN NOW. I MUST KEEP THIS DATE OR EVERYTHING I'VE WORKED FOR WILL BE WASTED, AND I CAN'T LET THAT HAPPEN . . .

Because I still remember the day I found her, hidden away in her shell.

H'MMM . . . NOW THERE'S SOMETHING THAT WOULD TAKE ANYONE'S MIND OFF THIS WINDY OLD BEACH. SHE'S PRETTY!

BEACH PHOTOGRAPHER. SMILE, PLEASE!

H-HUH? NO THANKS . . . I'M NOT INTERESTED.

NO . . . I DON'T THINK SO. I REALLY DON'T THINK YOU COULD.

But that didn't stop me trying . . .

COFFEE'S ALWAYS NICER OUT OF A FLASK, BUT I KNOW A GREAT LITTLE CAFE THAT DOES BACON ROLLS. WE COULD MEET IN TOWN AND . . .

I'D RATHER NOT, JIMMY. I'D RATHER JUST STAY HERE.

OH, YES, YOU'VE BEEN HURT SOMEWHERE ALONG THE LINE. AND YOU'RE NOT GOING TO TAKE THE CHANCE OF IT HAPPENING AGAIN, ARE YOU?

GOING TO A DISCO OR THE CINEMA OR EVEN JUST A CAFE MEANS A REAL DATE. AND REAL DATES LEAD TO REAL TEARS . . . I KNOW . . .

That was why we only ever met on the beach. But we saw each other there often after that. And two things happened very quickly—she became my friend . . .

HE DIED NOT FAR FROM HERE, YOU SEE. A BOATING ACCIDENT. WE'D BEEN ENGAGED ONLY A FEW MONTHS.

HE'D MADE SO MANY PROMISES ABOUT ALL THE THINGS WE'D DO TOGETHER. NONE OF THEM CAME TRUE . . .

AND YOU HIDE HERE NOW, SO NO- ONE ELSE WILL EVER HAVE THE CHANCE TO MAKE YOU PROMISES. OR BREAK THEM.

19

YES. BUT DON'T BE SAD ABOUT IT, JIMMY. I'M NOT.

THAT'S THE SADDEST THING OF ALL, CHRISTINE. IT'S AS IF YOU STOPPED LIVING WHEN HE DID.

And I fell in love with her . . .

ANOTHER PHOTO? WHY D'YOU TAKE SO MANY OF ME?

BECAUSE I WANT TO CAPTURE YOU, TO MAKE YOU MINE. YOU ONLY LET ME DO IT WITH PHOTOGRAPHS.

BUT ALWAYS IN BLACK AND WHITE. WHY?

BECAUSE THAT'S ALL YOU ARE TO ME, CHRISTINE. JUST BLACK AND WHITE.

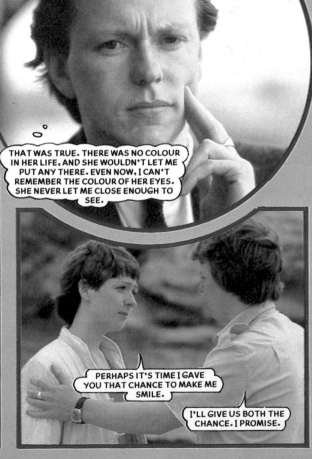

THAT WAS TRUE. THERE WAS NO COLOUR IN HER LIFE, AND SHE WOULDN'T LET ME PUT ANY THERE. EVEN NOW, I CAN'T REMEMBER THE COLOUR OF HER EYES. SHE NEVER LET ME CLOSE ENOUGH TO SEE.

Until one day . . .

I CAN'T GO ON LIKE THIS, CHRISTINE. WE HAVE TO MEET IN OTHER PLACES. YOU HAVE TO EXIST SOMEWHERE OTHER THAN THIS BEACH!

PERHAPS YOU'RE RIGHT, JIMMY . . .

PERHAPS IT'S TIME I GAVE YOU THAT CHANCE TO MAKE ME SMILE.

I'LL GIVE US BOTH THE CHANCE. I PROMISE.

Blue Jeans Beauty

An at-a-glance guide to skin care

# SKIN-FORMATION

## face facts

SKIN consists of three layers. The lowest layer is fatty tissue which gives your face its smooth outline. The middle layer contains sweat glands, hair follicles, blood vessels and nerve endings.

The top layer is made up of five thinner layers of skin cells. The lowest of these is moist and plump, but as they move up to the surface they dry out, and once at the surface they die and flake off.

Since they're continually being replaced this doesn't matter — but if the dead skin is left on the surface too long, it can block your pores and cause blemishes.

So, it's important to cleanse, tone and moisturise to clear away dirt and skin debris and keep your face soft.

## all about cleansers

CREAM CLEANSER — suits normal to dry skin. A thick one is best for end-of-the-day removing of make-up, while a lighter one's good for morning clean-ups.

Apply it in upward, circular movements, but don't rub it in hard since that only pushes dirt further into your pores!

LIQUID CLEANSER — suits normal to oily skin. If you're prone to spots, go for a medicated one. Tip a little on to a cotton-wool ball and wipe it over your face until no more dirt comes away.

CLEANSING PADS — are pieces of material soaked in cleanser. Handy to wipe away oil and dirt when travelling or away from home.

CLEANSING GRAINS — are tiny granules which you mix with water and rub into your face to get rid of dead surface skin cells and stubborn dirt. NOT to be used on dry or delicate skin — but they can help clear a spotty one.

SOAP AND WATER — is still a good way of cleaning skin, particularly if it's on the oily side. Don't use *any* soap, though — stick to a mild one, like baby soap, or one described as suitable for your complexion. Avoid any which're strongly-scented or with added deodorant.

Work up a good lather in your hands before you smooth it on to your face, then rinse the suds off thoroughly with lots of warm water. Blot your face dry with a towel — don't rub — and if your skin feels at all "tight", smooth on a layer of moisturiser.

FACIAL SAUNA — can help a lot if your skin is oily or blemished, as it opens pores and loosens spots and blackheads.

Fill a bowl with hot water and hold your face about ten inches above. Cover your head and the basin with a towel to keep the steam in — and just let that moist atmosphere go to work on your face!

Stop after five minutes, clean your face with your normal cleanser, then splash on a toner.

EYE MAKE-UP REMOVER — is a specially mild cleanser. It gets rid of stubborn make-up without lots of rubbing which could drag the delicate skin around your eyes.

## all about toners

ASTRINGENT — is the choice for oily skin. It contains lots of alcohol so is most effective at getting rid of grease. After you've cleansed your face, pour a little astringent on to a cotton-wool pad and wipe it over your skin. If the pad looks dirty, keep doing it till it's clean. Your face'll feel tingling fresh.

TONER — is best for normal skin as it's milder than astringent, but still clears away any traces of cleanser which could make your skin look greasy if left behind.

SKIN FRESHENER — is the mildest and so the best for dry skin. If your face is VERY dry, you can dilute it by dampening your cotton-wool with water first.

## all about moisturisers

MOISTURISER — is essential for all skin types as it protects your face from the roughening effects of sun, wind, heat, cold, etc. It seals moisture (i.e. water) into your skin to keep it soft, and prevents dirt from sinking in too deep.

Oily skin needs a light, milky one; normal skin a medium, creamy one — and dry skin a thicker, rich, ultra-creamy one. Smooth it on to slightly damp skin for the best results.

EYE CREAM — like neck cream, this really isn't necessary for young skins. When you reach your late twenties it helps keep wrinkles at bay — but don't waste your money on it yet.

LIP SALVE — invaluable for everyone! It softens lips and prevents them becoming dry and cracked. Wear it on its own or under lipstick.

## all about masks

FACE MASKS — come in loads of different forms but they all do much the same job. They draw dirt out from your pores, loosen blackheads and freshen your skin. They also tone up your circulation, giving your face a healthy glow — and remove dead surface skin cells, leaving your face with a smoother, softer surface.

Whatever problem you have, there's a mask to help it — just read the details on the pack. But bear in mind that they can unsettle your skin and make it a bit blotchy for a time before the benefits can really be seen — so it's not a good idea to use one just before you go anywhere special! Try it the night — or even week — before.

When applying a mask, avoid the delicate skin around your eyes and mouth — and relax somewhere private!

# Diary Of A Failed Dieter!
## She Knows Everything About The Fats Of Life!

I KNOW it's going to work. OK, so I failed the grapefruit and yoghurt diet, but that's because Christmas Eve's not a good time to start a grapefruit and yoghurt diet, is it? And I failed the counting calories diet, 'cos maths never was my best subject, and I failed the starvation diet when the noises from my rumbling tum drowned out the records at the disco . . . but I'm not going to fail this one, 'cos I spent a whole week's pocket money on the book. "Thinner Sinners" by Dr Slim, it's called, and it's foolproof.

*I KNOW SALADS AREN'T FATTENING, BUT....!*

First thing you do, is think beautiful thoughts about being thin, on a beautiful morning when the birds're all twittering and the sun's shining.

And this morning, when I opened my eyes, the sun was shining right on my spare tyre.

"I'm thin! I'm beautiful!" I whispered to it, all dreamily. I had this great dream about floating in Sting's arms and he's telling me I'm light as a feather . . .

"You *ever* going to get up?" Mum yelled. Ten past eight! Not a good start when the bus leaves at quarter past. Quick dive into uniform, a couple of swigs of Mum's cold coffee, a fistful of clammy toast, and I'm off, chugging my chubby body down the road, thinking thin, chewing my toast.

"A brisk walk, or healthy trot for a mile or two helps tighten a tubby tummy!" Dr Slim says. I reckon my hundred-yard dash qualifies as tummy-tightener. After all, it feels like a mile or two to me, and Dr Slim says it's what you feel like that counts.

I feel like a big helping of cornflakes with a can of strawberries poured on the top, finished off with a dollop of cream, egg and bacon to follow, and some hot muffins oozing butter. They don't serve that on our school bus, though — and anyway, I'm on this diet.

"I'm on this diet!" I keep telling everyone all morning. Tell your friends, Dr Slim advises. It'll boost your confidence.

"Bet that won't last long!" Julie says. Some confidence boosting! Julie's a tall pin so she doesn't need to think thin. She has problems stopping herself falling down drains. But she's not bad really. She sees that she's let me down, and shares her sandwiches with me before I go into school lunch to cheer me up.

I think I'm allowed the sandwiches, 'cos there was cucumber on them, and that's so thin you can see through it. There was cheese and peanut butter on them as well and salmon spread, but that's just energy food, and I need all the energy I can get hold of if I'm going to resist the chips and have salad for lunch.

The sandwiches really help. I make straight for the salads and heap a great pile on my plate, because Dr Slim says salad food isn't fattening.

It doesn't look too good, though, all that green. But it looks better when I've brightened it up with tomato ketchup, salad cream, brown sauce, yellow pickles, six pickled onions and some potato salad.

I dream thin dreams right through English, and feel much better. I feel very thin until Julie yells at home time. "Are we going for the bus, or d'you want me to roll you home?"

"I'm walking!" I say, huffily.

A brisk walk. I need a brisk walk with friends like mine! I mean, the only way to stop Julie showing me up is to walk briskly away from her.

I'm upset tonight, 'cos she stops to talk to Kevin Gray and I have to hang around, more like a green beach-ball than a gooseberry. I hang around in the direction of the sweet shop, just to pass the time, and find myself buying half a pound of wine gums. Well, they're drink, not food, aren't they? I've finished them all by the time Julie's stopped chatting Kevin Gray up.

"C'mon!" I snap at her.

"Oh, stop throwing your weight around!" she giggles.

That does it! I clump off home, determined to show her I can do it when I try. I can, too. I can on the days when Mum's not made one of her big roast dinners with jam roly-poly for pudding. This isn't one of those days, and anyway, I'm starving after that salad lunch.

"Seconds?" Mum asks when she sees my eyes glued on the last little bit of roly-poly that's left over.

"Only small seconds. I'm on this diet!" I say, nobly, flashing out my plate before Dad grabs the left-overs.

Tomorrow's going to be better. Tomorrow I'll start thinking about a new diet.

And today wasn't too bad. After all, I lost three pounds — that's what Dr Slim's foolproof book cost me!

## Puzzle Pics

Feeling clever? Then bend your mind to these four Puzzle Pics, and see if you can guess what the objects in the photos are. We've given you a few clues to get you started, but if you really get stuck the answers are at the bottom of the page.

1. Sounds a bit slippery.

2. Pretty girls get the wolf variety!

3. Monkeys love them.

**Answers:**
1. A chute. 2. A whistle. 3. A banana.

## BLUE BEAD CHOKER

Simply thread your own choice of chunky beads (try looking in junk shops and jumble sales for old necklaces you can salvage beads from) on to a length of leather thonging or ribbon!

## SUPER SPIRALS

Take a piece of medium fuse wire about 5 inches long, thread a bead on, bend the end up, then slide the next bead over the two ends of wire — see Fig. A.

Thread on your choice of beads till you've covered about 4 inches and twist the remaining piece of wire round an earring base (available from good craft shops).

Wind the length of beads around your finger to make the spiral.

A nice idea is to make a ring to match — just thread beads on to a double thickness of shirring elastic, tie the ends together and tuck them away inside the beads.

# BEAD-DAZZLED!

That's what everyone'll be when they see you in these great bead earrings 'n' things. We're about to show you how to make them, too — so just look 'ear!

## FALLING RAINDROPS

These delicate earrings are made by threading a bead on to a 5-inch length of fuse wire, securing as in Fig. A, then adding a large, transparent pear-shaped one followed by clear bugle beads spaced out with tiny blue ones. Finally, twist the last bit of wire round an earring base.

## CRAZY HOOPS

Take a 9-inch length of fuse wire and thread on three yellow beads, three orange ones, three yellow ones, and so on till you've covered about 7½ inches of it. Keep hold of both ends all the time so the beads don't slide off.

Twist the two ends together to secure, then make the resulting circle into a figure of eight. Bring the two circles together and bind them with the spare wire ends.

Curl the remaining wire up tightly, glue it to the earring base with Bostik, then cover that with a large star sequin.

## TWISTERS

Take a piece of fuse wire about 7 inches long and cover 2 inches with tiny beads in one colour. Next, thread on one large bead, then cover 4 inches with tiny beads in a second colour.

Keeping hold of both ends, bend the wire at the large bead and wind the second coloured length tightly round the first. Wind the two ends of wire together to secure at the top, then fix to an earring base.

## CURLED FLOWER

Start with a large bead secured as before to the end of a 6-inch length of fuse wire. Thread on enough medium-sized, differently-coloured beads to circle round it.

Fill the rest of the length with small beads in a third colour, and attach the end of the wire to an earring base.

Then curl the beads tightly round the large one, as you can see in the pic.

## SWEET DROPS

Thread a large bead on to a 4-inch length of fuse wire and secure it as in Fig. A. Thread on four more large, round beads, followed by one small bead, several white bugle beads and another small bead (these little round ones stop the bugle beads just sliding down inside the larger beads!).

Finally, add one more large bead then twist the remaining wire round an earring base.

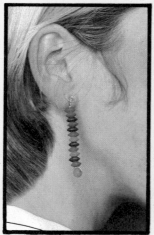

## CONCERTINA

Made in exactly the same way as "Sweet Drops," this earring uses flat, round beads for an unusual effect.

## LEAFY CLIP

This is the easiest of the lot! Loads of craft shops sell these tiny glass charms for adding to a bracelet or necklace. We simply glued one to an earring base with Bostik.

fig. A.

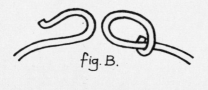

fig. B.

## TWISTED NECKLACE

It's so easy — and cheap — to make a necklace in your favourite colours, using beads and wire!

For this one, cut a piece of thick fuse wire long enough to fit snugly round your neck, plus an inch or two for the catch at the back.

Thread on enough beads to cover that, then bend the ends into a "hook and eye" type of fastening. See Fig. B.

Take a piece of thinner fuse wire about the same length and cover it with beads in a contrasting colour. Wind one wire end tightly round the main necklace about 4 inches from the fastening, then twist the second colour round the first till you reach a point 4 inches from the other end.

Twist the second wire tightly round the main necklace as before.

## Monkeying Around

You're a cheery, outgoing personality and you'll do just about anything for a laugh! People love to have you around when they're feeling a bit down — nobody could really be miserable for long in your company!

You're quite ambitious, but you'll have no problem climbing the ladder of success!

# Animal

## The Cat's Whiskers

If the cat was your choice, then we reckon you're probably a contented, home-loving purrson who likes nothing better than to curl up in front of a cosy fire and relax! You're inclined to have rather a high opinion of yourself sometimes, so don't keep trying to convince everyone you're the cat's whiskers!

You tend to take risks but you'd be wise to remember that, unlike our feline friend here, YOU don't have nine lives!

## Going To The Dogs!

You like your fella to be masterful, all right, but you shouldn't always be quite so ready to come to heel every time he calls!

You're usually pretty easy-going but when you DO lose your temper, everyone had better look out! It's just as well your friends know your bark's always worse than your bite!

## The Boy Of Her Dreams

*A Special Mini-Story By Barbara Jacobs*

I STOOD, red-nosed and shivering on the cinema steps, hating Frankie for being late again. In a few minutes he'd come racing round that windswept corner, all out of breath with his cheeky smiles and gulped apologies, and I'd tell him. I'd tell him that I was sick and tired of the crazy unpredictability I'd once found so attractive.

I'd found Paul, now. He was really smooth. So I'd prepared the exact words I was going to say to Frankie when he tried his flip-flop smile on me. I was going to say, "It's no use. I've decided. You're just not smooth. A very lovely young typist, like me, needs a guy who's smooth enough to appreciate her."

Frankie was so unsmooth that he was fuzzy round the edges. His moppy chestnut curls were fuzzy, his frayed jeans were fuzzy, his unravelled Dr Who scarf fuzzed twice round his neck and his eyes were fuzzy most of the time with laughter or tears or dreams.

# Magnetism!

Follow your animal instincts to see which of these pictures you're drawn to, then read on to find out what sort of creature YOU really are!

## Feeling Sheepish?

On the surface, you're a pretty meek character, but you're not afraid to stand up for yourself if the need arises. However, you (or is it ewe?!) should watch out for people who might try to take advantage of your good nature.

Instead of just going along with the crowd, try to follow the example of somebody you really admire.

## Pig In The Middle

It doesn't take much to make you happy, as a rule! You're always inclined to put things off till tomorrow — and somehow, tomorrow never seems to come! In other words, you're lazy!

Try not to take sides in an argument, but just watch you don't get caught in the crossfire!

You can be generous to a fault and your mates often turn to you for help and advice. They reckon a grunt of approval from you means a lot!

---

And none of his dreams ever came true.

But my dreams did. I'd worked hard at my first-ever job — dressed neatly, acted efficiently and applied for promotion to Head Office, into a sparkly new office with only one other girl, Jeannie, to be part of the two-girl typing pool for the sales reps. It was a fantastic job, a dream come true.

"Sweet, practical Laura," crazy Frankie called me, pinging the top of my neat nose with a flick of his finger and thumb. Huh! Paul hadn't seen me that way at all.

"What's a very lovely typist like you doing in a very tatty pool like this?" he'd asked me, when we met for the first time this morning.

"Watch him!" Jeannie had winked at me. "That's Paul. He's a smoothie!"

"Just what I need!" I'd murmured, smoothing my smooth jersey skirt over my smooth knees. I was still stunned by the clear blue eyes and clean-cut smile.

"Don't do it, little Red Riding Hood!" Jeannie laughed. She'd already admired my new red mac. "That particular wolf's got very big eyes, but even bigger teeth!"

"Well . . ." I'd faltered.

But I wasn't faltering now. I'd made up my mind. Fuzzy Frankie didn't go with my new image.

"I'll take you to the flicks to celebrate your first day at the new office," he'd said on Saturday, and I'd asked, "What time? And how late will you be?"

"Seven. And I won't!" he'd told me, all brown-eyed sincerity. I should've known better. Art students, it seemed, were always stuck into lumps of clay when you needed them most.

I wiped a very untypical, impractical tear out of one eye, and glanced up at the Town Hall clock. Half past seven.

And right on cue, just in time to miss the tear, he came hurtling round the corner, a multi-coloured, panting mass of curls, grins and gulped excuses, holding something behind his back.

"Sorry, Loopy!" he sighed, sliding to a stop. He called me Loopy when he was very, very sorry. "I stopped to pick you a chrysanthemum out of the park!"

He offered me one droopy stem with enormous elegance, and then collapsed into giggles. "Well, look at that!" he spluttered. "You've blown his mind. He's lost his head over you, just like I have!"

I had to laugh. I just had to, expecially when he stuck the headless chrysan-themum behind my ear, and knelt down on the cinema steps to kiss my frozen hand. His glow of warmth and energy and humour was infectious.

Smoothie Paul suddenly seemed like frosted sugar on the rim of an empty glass.

I felt silly, and stupidly in love with a mad idiot who smiled like summer sunshine.

"Guess what?" he laughed. "Treat's only just beginning! Flicks are out tonight. I've cooked some special burned spaghetti and a can of Coke for you. Celebration dinner! And I'd like you to look at a little silver ring I've been making. It might just fit one of your fingers."

His voice had softened to a husky whisper. My eyes had opened wider than Red Riding Hood's.

"What?" I gulped.

"I need a sweet, practical girl with her feet on the ground," he whispered, flicking me a heart-stopping wink.

And I had to admit, as I fell against his fuzzy jacket and into his warm arms, that I needed a boy whose eyes were fuzzy, most of the time, with laughter, or tears, or dreams.

## Toyah Wilcox:

"Being the only girl is something I've learnt to forget about. If I emphasised the fact that I'm female, then I'd get treated like one — and I couldn't bear that!

"I do get a bit of extra privacy, though, which is marvellous because when you're touring that's something you learn to value.

"The band respect me — but I think that's because I work pretty hard. I don't look for an easier time just 'cos I'm a girl."

# GUYS AND DOLL

These top ladies of rock tell us what it's like to be the only girl in a band full of guys.

## Debbie Harry, Blondie:

"Well, I've got the great advantage of having Chris, my boyfriend, in the band.

"That makes things a lot easier and I think there are a lot of benefits in being together.

"I don't know if I could cope with being the only female — and the centre of attraction — if it wasn't for him.

"People do try to manipulate you more when you're a girl and they won't accept that women can have shrewd business minds, too, so sometimes they try to underpay you. At times like that I must admit I leave the talking to Chris!"

## Fay Fife, The Revillos:

"Being the only girl can have lots of advantages. For instance, you are immediately the centre of attraction. The disadvantage is that you're often put into the position of being asked to use the fact that you're female to sell the band.

"I'm often asked to do photo sessions without the other members of the group and I try to avoid that at all costs."

## Chrissie Hynde, The Pretenders:

"I've never really thought about being the only girl. You see, I've always been a bit of a tomboy and fellas have usually been my best mates.

"I hate females who flutter around, twittering a lot of silly nonsense whenever a bloke enters the room — and believe you me, there are a lot of them in show business!"

## Thereze Bazar, Dollar:

"I don't feel that it's very fair asking me this question. Our relationship isn't purely for business — it's pleasure, too!

"Mind you, even David has to admit that sometimes it can be much tougher for the girl in the band.

"I mean, when we're preparing for a tour, David just throws a few shirts and things into a small suitcase, while I struggle with hundreds of bottles of cleansers, liquids and stuff!"

## Annie Lennox:

"I don't feel like I'm the only girl in the band. I'm just me and they're just them and we're all a unit!

"I think surviving in this business is all down to your personality — and I can speak up for myself when I have to.

"The only time I'm aware of being different from the other group members is when the photographers all cluster round me and totally ignore the fellas. That really annoys me!"

## Pauline Black, The Selecter:

"Well, I suppose it seems slightly odd being the only girl travelling around with six fellas, but they don't give me any preferential treatment.

"To them, I'm just another musician and one of their mates. And that's the way I want it to stay — I couldn't stand it if they suddenly started opening doors for me and treating me like a real high and mighty lady!"

## Lene Lovich:

"I honestly never feel special in any way 'cos I'm the only female in the band. In fact, during the auditions, I didn't intend to choose male musicians — that's just the way it worked out.

"The only real difficulty arises when we're touring and we're all thrown into one tiny dressing-room. That means I have to grab all my gear and change in the ladies' loo!"

## Wendy Wu, The Photos:

"I must admit that being the only girl can cause a lot of silly arguments.

"I mean, some folk seem to think that I'm a bit stupid and can't give an intelligent opinion just 'cos I'm female.

"Although we all get on very well, I tend to spend quite a lot of time on my own. I think the guys would feel a bit edgy if I hung around with them all the time. And besides, I'm not usually interested in what they're talking about — unless it's music, of course!"

27

# THE DATING GAME

*Got a special date tonight? Well, don't panic! Just follow our beauty countdown and you'll soon be looking great!*

Don't dash off to get ready just yet. Give yourself at least twenty minutes breathing space. Read a magazine or make yourself a quick cuppa — w h i c h e v e r appeals to you most. Or if you're feeling really exhausted, lie back with a couple of slices of cucumber over your eyes. But don't be caught napping. You've loads to do before your date arrives!

**6·00**

Time to get up and go! Start running a warm bath, adding a splash of your favourite bath oil to the running water. Meanwhile, take out the outfit you plan to wear and check for loose buttons or split seams. If it needs pressing, a nice idea's to spray a little perfume on to the ironing board. The heat of the iron'll release the fragrance and delicately perfume your clothes.

**6·20**

Tie your hair back and cleanse your skin thoroughly. Splash on some skin freshener, then dot some moisturiser over your face and gently massage it in. Step into the bath and lather up all over. No long, hot soaks, though, 'cos this'll really dry out your skin and leave you feeling hot and flustered.

**6·30**

Towel yourself dry, and dust your body lightly with talc. Apply some anti-perspirant and wait a few minutes for it to dry. Now give your hair a quick wash, making sure you rinse it thoroughly. If time's short,

**6·45**

Blue Jeans Beauty

the next best thing's a dry shampoo powder, or try dabbing greasy roots with cotton wool soaked in eau-de-cologne.

If the top you're wearing pulls on over your head, put it on now. This way, you'll avoid messing up your hair and make-up later on. Blow dry your hair so it's fresh and swingy. If your hair's very fine, a light squish of hairspray'll help hold it in place.

**6·55**

If you're not going to be eating till later in the evening, fill up now with a glass of milk or fresh orange juice. Milk's best, 'cos it'll help to settle those pre-date nerves.
This is also a good time to paint your nails. Take off the old layer and repaint them with your favourite polish — making sure the colour doesn't clash with your special outfit. Or if you'd prefer, try using a nail buffer instead, for a pretty, natural look.
Finally massage in a blob of hand cream to make your hands really nice to hold.

**7·05**

Give your teeth a quick brush then face up to making-up. Dot on a little foundation and blend it smoothly over your face.
Keep your eye make-up subtle (especially if it's a first date) and resist the temptation to try out any zany new looks —

**7·15**

if you haven't practised first it could be disastrous. Smudge a little blusher along your cheekbones, blending it up and out with your fingertips. And finally slick a little coloured lip gloss over your lips for a pretty, pouting mouth.

Comb your hair into style. Then refresh your breath with a quick squirt of breath freshener. Pop this into your bag just in case you want it later on, and quickly check the contents of your bag to make sure you've everything you'll need.

**7·30**

Spray some of your favourite perfume behind your ears and on the insides of your wrists — but don't overdo it! Remember that you very quickly become accustomed to your own perfume, so what seems quite subtle to you may be overpowering to everyone else.

**7·40**

Clammy hand problem? Well, don't worry! Try holding them under cold water for a few minutes, then dry them off and rub a little anti-perspirant or talc into the palms. This should help keep them fresh.

**7·45**

Finally, put on your clothes and take a look in a full - length mirror — not forgetting to check the back view as well as the front one. Perfect! Well, what did you expect? Have a great time.

**7·50**

31

# No Matter What I Have To Do!

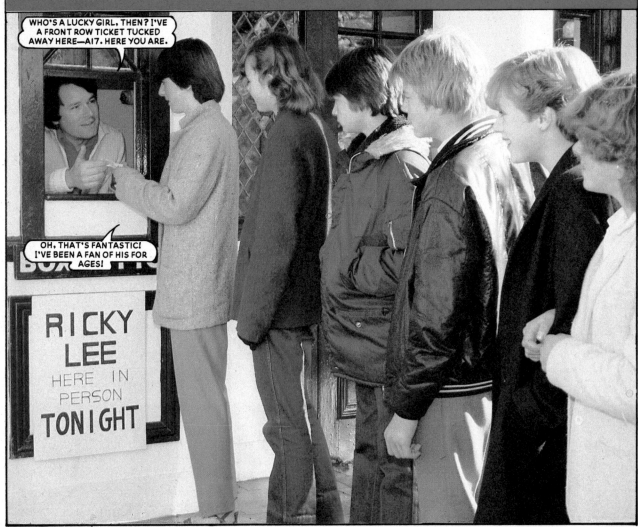

THAT'S...ER...WHAT I WANTED TO TALK ABOUT, JEAN. YOU SEE, I'M NOT GETTING ANYWHERE HERE, LOVE. SO I THOUGHT I'D CHANCE MY LUCK AND GO TO LONDON. THAT IS...IF YOU DON'T MIND BEING LEFT ON YOUR OWN FOR A BIT?

MIND? OF COURSE I DON'T MIND! THAT'S THE MOST SENSIBLE THING YOU'VE EVER SAID. LONDON'S WHERE THE BIG TIME IS—AND THAT'S WHERE THEY'LL REALLY APPRECIATE YOU.

OH, THANKS, JEAN—FOR BEING SO UNDERSTANDING. I WAS TERRIFIED YOU WERE GOING TO BURST INTO TEARS, OR SOMETHING!

And so, a few days later . . .

WHEN I COME BACK I'LL BE FAMOUS, LOVE. THEN WE'LL GET MARRIED AND I'LL BUY YOU ALL THE THINGS I'VE ALWAYS WANTED TO, BUT COULDN'T AFFORD.

RICKY, I DON'T WANT PRESENTS. I JUST WANT YOU TO GET THE SUCCESS YOU DESERVE. AND WHEN YOU COME BACK HERE, A STAR, YOU'LL FIND ME WAITING FOR YOU IN A17—WHATEVER HAPPENS!

But, after Ricky had gone . . .

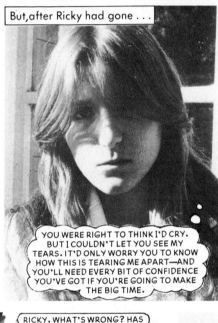

YOU WERE RIGHT TO THINK I'D CRY. BUT I COULDN'T LET YOU SEE MY TEARS. IT'D ONLY WORRY YOU TO KNOW HOW THIS IS TEARING ME APART—AND YOU'LL NEED EVERY BIT OF CONFIDENCE YOU'VE GOT IF YOU'RE GOING TO MAKE THE BIG TIME.

To begin with, letters from Ricky came thick and fast . . .

"YES, I'M EATING ALL THE FRESH FRUIT I CAN, JUST LIKE I PROMISED YOU. THE GUYS IN THE DIGS SAY I'LL BE THE HEALTHIEST UNEMPLOYED SINGER IN THE BUSINESS!" OH, RICKY—IT'S GREAT TO KNOW YOU'RE NOT LOSING HEART.

And then, one day, Jean got a surprise phone call . . .

HELLO, LOVE, I'VE GOT SOMETHING TO TELL YOU.

RICKY, WHAT'S WRONG? HAS SOMETHING HAPPENED?

SOMETHING'S HAPPENED ALL RIGHT —SOMETHING GREAT! I THINK I'VE GOT THAT BREAK I WAS AFTER. I'M PLAYING IN A BIG CONCERT TONIGHT, AND IF THE CRITICS LIKE ME—I'M IN! WISH ME LUCK!

OH, THAT'S WONDERFUL, RICKY. I'LL KEEP MY FINGERS CROSSED FOR YOU—AND FOR US AND OUR FUTURE!

And next morning . . .

FANTASTIC! RICKY'S DONE IT! IT SAYS HERE THAT A NEW STAR IS BORN AND HIS NAME IS RICKY LEE. MY RICKY . . . I ALWAYS KNEW HE'D MAKE IT . . .

And Ricky went on climbing the ladder of success, until . . .

AND NOW THE SOUND YOU ALL WANT TO HEAR. IT'S NUMBER ONE—RICKY LEE SINGING ACHING HEART BLUES!

IT'S LIKE A DREAM COME TRUE! THE WHOLE WORLD'S GOING MAD FOR RICKY. HEY—THAT SOUNDED LIKE THE POST ARRIVING!

NOTHING FROM RICKY, THOUGH—JUST A ROTTEN OLD BILL. BUT IT'S NO WONDER HE HASN'T BEEN WRITING SO OFTEN LATELY. HE MUST BE REALLY BUSY NOW . . .

But, as the months dragged by, the letters became even fewer. Then, one day . . .

RICKY'S COMING HERE! OH, I'M SO EXCITED! IT'S BEEN AGES SINCE I'VE SEEN HIM. I'D BETTER GET MY TICKET RIGHT NOW, BEFORE THEY SELL OUT.

And . . .

I GOT IT—I GOT A17, JUST LIKE I PROMISED RICKY! BUT WHY WAIT TILL THE CONCERT TO SEE HIM? I'LL GO DOWN TO THE STATION BEFOREHAND AND WAIT TILL HIS TRAIN COMES IN.

And on the day . . .

SMILE, PLEASE, MR LEE.

THERE'S RICKY—HE HASN'T CHANGED A BIT. HE WENT AWAY TO MAKE HIS FORTUNE SO WE COULD GET MARRIED AND HE'S DONE JUST THAT.

THANKS, MR LEE.

SO NOW WE CAN HAVE THAT HOME FOR TWO WE'VE ALWAYS DREAMED OF. JUST RICKY AND ME—AND ALL THE LOVE IN THE WORLD.

JEAN!

WELCOME HOME, LOVE. LOOK, I'VE KEPT MY PROMISE. I TOLD YOU I'D BE WAITING FOR YOU IN A17 WHATEVER HAPPENED—AND AS YOU CAN SEE, I WILL BE.

... THIS IS ZELDA. MY FIANCEE.

NO, RICKY, NO! HOW COULD YOU DO THIS TO ME? AFTER ALL WE'VE MEANT TO EACH OTHER—TO GET ENGAGED TO ANOTHER GIRL WITHOUT EVEN TELLING ME!

OH, RICKY, I'M SO GLAD YOU'RE HOME. I'VE MISSED YOU TERRIBLY! BUT EVERYTHING'S GOING TO BE SO WONDERFUL NOW—IT WAS WORTH WAITING FOR.

JEAN ... I DON'T KNOW HOW TO SAY THIS, BUT ...

DON'T RUN AWAY, JEAN! PLEASE! COME BACK—LET ME EXPLAIN!

But Jean ran on, her eyes blinded by tears ...

JEAN, LOOK WHERE YOU'RE GOING! LOOK OUT FOR THAT LORRY!

AA-A-GH!

OH, N-NO, POOR JEAN! IF ONLY I'D HAD THE COURAGE TO TELL HER ABOUT ZELDA BEFORE. BUT INSTEAD I LEFT IT TOO LATE—AND BECAUSE OF THAT SHE'S DEAD! TH- THIS IS ALL MY FAULT!

But the show must go on, and at the end of the concert that night ...

GREAT, RICKY!

BRAVO!

ENCORE!

THEY'RE LOVING ME OUT THERE—BUT WHAT DOES THAT MEAN TO ME? ALL I CAN SEE IS A17, THE ONE EMPTY SEAT IN THE HOUSE—WHERE JEAN USED TO SIT AND ENCOURAGE ME WHEN NO-ONE ELSE EVEN KNEW I EXISTED!

But then . . .

NO, IT CAN'T BE HAPPENING! IT JUST ISN'T POSSIBLE! IT'S JEAN—SHE'S SITTING OUT THERE IN THE AUDIENCE—IN A17!

DEAR RICKY, WHEN I SAID I'D BE HERE WHATEVER HAPPENED—I MEANT IT! NOT EVEN DEATH CAN KEEP US APART!

WELL, THAT'S THE STORY—APART FROM THE FACT THAT EVERY TIME RICKY APPEARS HERE NOW, JEAN'S ALWAYS SITTING IN A17, LOOKING UP AT HIM.

WHAT A HORRIBLE STORY!

HEY, WHAT'RE YOU DOING?

BOX OFFICE

RICKY LEE
HERE IN PERSON
TONIGHT

GETTING RID OF THIS TICKET! IF YOU THINK I'M SHARING ANY SEAT WITH A GHOST, YOU'VE GOT ANOTHER THINK COMING!

YOU, THERE—WHAT'S ALL THAT RUBBISH ABOUT RICKY LEE AND JEAN? EVERYBODY KNOWS THEY GOT MARRIED AS SOON AS HE BECAME FAMOUS, AND ARE STILL TOGETHER AS HAPPY AS EVER. SO, WHY ALL THOSE LIES ABOUT HER GETTING KILLED AND THEN HAUNTING RICKY?

BOX OFFICE

RICKY LEE
HERE IN PERSON
TONIGHT

IT'S QUITE SIMPLE, REALLY . . .

I'VE NEVER MISSED A RICKY LEE CONCERT IN MY LIFE—AND WHAT'S MORE, I DON'T INTEND TO. NO MATTER WHAT I HAVE TO DO TO GET A TICKET!

LITTLE THEATRE
RICKY LEE
JAN 3RD
7:30
A17

**THE END**

WHEN someone's all set to throw a party, is your name first on the invites list? Or are you always the last to know? Try our quiz to find out whether you're the life and soul of the party — or just a dead loss!

1. There's a ding-dong on your door-bell and you trot off, expecting to see the Avon lady — but no!

There're six hundred (well, seems like it!) folk standing there, blowing party tooters, wearing silly hats and shrieking, "Hey! This where the party's at?" Do you . . .
a. holler "NO!" above all the noise and slam the door in their silly faces?
b. fall to the floor in a faint and get trampled underfoot in the rush?
c. zoom off to the kitchen to prepare six hundred sausages an' pickled onions on sticks?

2. You've been persuaded (fool that you are!) to take along some sounds to this party. Halfway through the revelry, you notice the DJ is using your fave Jam album to stand his collection of fruit punch glasses on. Do you . . .
a. whip away your album and empty all fifteen glasses over his head?
b. search out **his** records and proceed to do a Travolta take-off on top of them?
c. sigh and reckon that's the price you pay for bringing it here?

3. Your best mate is on the way to becoming your worst enemy, 'cos she's practising her Debbie Harry act on the guy you fancy. She's all pout and fluttering lashes in his face!

But meanwhile, you're trapped in a corner with Fat Fred who obviously fancies his chances with *you*. What d'you do?
a. Look daggers in her direction.
b. Be kind to Freddie for the meantime. In ten minutes you'll saunter across and knock that hunk's socks off with one devastating smile – no contest!
c. Holler across the room at your mate, "Watch out, Mavis! Your girdle's giving way!"

4. This bloke has been tucking into too much Tizer and cramming sausage rolls down his neck for two solid hours.

Suddenly, he sprints past you in the direction of the loo, looking decidedly green! Do you . . .
a. hare off after him, ready to do your Florence Nightingale bit?
b. stick out a foot to trip him up and snigger as he rolls around on the floor in agony?
c. distract everyone else from the poor fella's plight, by suggesting you turn down the lights for a bit of smoochy dancing?

5. Some twit's suggested a game of Postie's Knock and every tasty guy in the room is paired off with one of your lucky pals. Come your turn, you're landed with (you guessed!) Fat Fred! So what d'you do?
a. Stamp your feet and thcream and thcream until you're thick! You didn't want to play thith game anyway!
b. Smile and let Freddie have a quick greasy peck at your cheek.
c. Trot off to powder your nose . . . and stay away for three hours till the coast's clear.

6. You're out in the back garden — stargazing, what else? — with your best friend's boy. The romance of the moment is too much for the poor bloke! He just has to grab you, take you in his arms and plant a long, loving smacker on your lips!

Just then, you notice that forty-two pairs of eyes are on you. That's right, the whole party's stopped to watch the passion! What *can* you do?
a. Grin and say, "Mavis is right, folks! He's the best kisser in the village!"
b. Pretend you haven't noticed and droop delicately back into his arms .
c. Stick out your tongue at 'em and say, "Beats scoffing cucumber sarnies and sitting in the corner!"

Well, d'you make parties sink or swing? Tot up your score to find out!

**SCORE**
1. a. 10  b. 0  c. 5
2. a. 5  b. 10  c. 0
3. a. 0  b. 5  c. 10
4. a. 0  b. 10  c. 5
5. a. 10  b. 5  c. 0
6. a. 5  b. 0  c. 10

## Conclusions

**45-60: Well, you make things sizzle all right, 'cos you're hot stuff!**

In fact, anyone who comes too close to you is likely to get their fingers burned! You're out to have a good time, sure — and you'll stamp all over anyone who gets in your way!

You're so selfish, you'd ruin someone else's fun, just so's you could have a giggle. But believe us, that's not funny. So if you can't get into the party spirit, stay away!

**25-40: Well done! You'd make the perfect party hostess! You like to see things going with a swing, and you're prepared to get out the elbow grease yourself to make sure they do!**

You know that a good party needs a bit of graft to make it go well, so you work at it. And you know that some folk need watching, so that things don't get too wild. Bet all your guests go away happy from one of your dos. Invite us to the next one, will you?!

**0-20: Well, you're not out to spoil the fun for anyone else, but you're not exactly a live wire! You'd be as much at home at a Sunday school picnic — and probably have more laughs!**

Take a tip from us — don't try to blend in with the wallpaper, next time you go to a knees-up! Get out there, join in the frolics — and enjoy yourself for once!

QUICK QUIZ

# are you QUEEN of the party scene?

38

*Neither of us would ever love anyone else . . .*

# Just A Few Empty Promises...

## *I'd heard all the stories about holiday romances but I was sure ours was different . . .*

I'D believed that Paul was more than just a summer love. I'd believed it so much that I'd blown my whole future on a few empty promises whispered into a summer wind.

At least, that's what everyone told me. They told me I was mad, crazy, out of my mind to go on believing and trusting. Eventually, I found myself starting to lose some of the faith that I'd had. All that was left then was loneliness.

Before the holiday, I'd been happy enough. Billy and I had drifted round together, a couple in the middle of a gang of friends, sharing all the familiar jokes, smiling at all the same old people.

I liked him, but I knew we wouldn't last for ever.

Somewhere in the back of my mind I thought we'd split up after the summer, when he started work and I started my secretarial course, and both of us met new friends. Maybe, if it happened like that, everything would've been easier.

Paul was unbelievable, and unexpected. Perhaps that's the way real love is, appearing out of nowhere and breaking your life up into little glittering pieces.

# Happiness

Or perhaps, as Mum kept telling me, it was just the excitement of holiday sunshine, moonlight walks, and the difference that being away from home brings.

Mum tried her best to dampen my enthusiasm right from the beginning, even though she admitted that Paul was a nice boy.

Nice! That's the understatement of the century. He wasn't great-looking. But he had the kind of face that smiled in unexpected places, that broke into sunshine whenever we looked at each other, that made my heart pound and my breath catch, a face that was funny and sad and serious and crazily alive with happiness.

From the first moment I saw him, standing in the doorway of his caravan, I knew he was the one I'd always loved.

I knew exactly what his voice would sound like, what he would say, how he would laugh, with his head thrown back and his eyes screwed up, and I knew he'd enjoy the

From the first moment, I knew he was the one I'd always loved.

Paul wasn't going to write. He'd forgotten all our promises.

We felt, on tha

things I enjoyed. And he didn't let me down.

Not then. Not on the holiday. We just fell readily in love, spent every second of every minute together, and felt, on that last day, as if part of ourselves would be lost for ever and ever, unless

we made the promises that would bind us together.

We clung to each other, and cried, and promised. Neither of us would ever love anyone else. This was for ever.

I cried all the way home in the car, while Mum sat with her lips

I had to live with the loneliness.

...ay, as if part of ourselves would be lost for ever and ever . . .

nothing at all.

No phone calls. No letters. And no address. I wrote to the site and asked for my letters to be forwarded, but there was no reply. Mum's lips pursed even more, Des kept giving me these little pitying looks and told me these holiday romances always end like that.

But my heart said something else. It told me to go on believing, to trust in the funny instinct that had drawn me to Paul in the first place. That instinct told me he wouldn't forget me. Some day, he'd find me again.

Meanwhile, I had to live with the loneliness. That was worse than anything I'd ever experienced in my life. I'd been used to being surrounded by friends.

## Outcast

Every evening, there'd been someone to talk to, somewhere to go, someone phoning or knocking at the door, the gang of girls at school who'd always listen if you wanted to let off steam, or cry on someone's shoulder. But I'd thrown it all away by falling in love with Paul.

I started at the Tech as an outcast. Debbie and Lynne and Evie were on the course as well, but they refused to speak to me. It took me a week to realise that it was because of the way I'd treated Billy.

I'd been stupid enough to think that it wouldn't make any difference to any of my own friends, but the turned backs and the silences and the hard, cold looks told me to think again.

Then Lynne finally said, right out, one day in that first week when I

pursed, saying nothing, and Des did his big brother act on me, sitting in the back of the car with his arm round me, telling me everything would be OK.

He told me how he'd fallen in love one year on holiday, but it hadn't lasted.

I took no notice of the pursed lips or Des's efforts to put me off, gently. I did what I had to do as soon as I got home. I finished with Billy, told the gang I wouldn't be around any more, and sat waiting for the telephone to ring.

It rang every night for

a fortnight, the whole fortnight that Paul stayed down on the site with his friends. And there were letters, too, letters I treasured, saying that as soon as they all came home he'd arrange to come over to visit me for a weekend.

Then, suddenly,

41

tried to sit at their table in the canteen, "Some people just don't know when they're not wanted, Cheryl Wilson! Can't you get the message? Billy's all broken up by what you've done to him, and he's going out with me now! So clear off!"

I didn't go to the shorthand class that afternoon. I went to sit in the park, to think things over. It didn't take an awful lot of working out, though I had no-one to blame, really, but myself.

That first crush of love had hit me so hard that I'd thrown away everything else, cut myself off completely from the things and the people who'd mattered to me before. Now I had nothing at all.

I'd hurt Billy and I'd disappointed my friends by not seeming to care that I'd hurt him. And all for nothing, for a feeling that had faded as quickly as sunshine.

I searched Paul's letters for comfort. I looked into the memories of that one magic week we'd spent together, and wondered if I'd imagined it all.

# Hopeless

I didn't really have much to go on, just endless, easy conversations, the trembling recollections of a touch of a finger slowly running the length of my arm, gentle lips brushing mine, fingers twined in my hair, laughter, sunshine, moonlight. Nothing special. Nothing to make up for losing everything else in my life.

"Well!" Mum kept saying as I waited for the postman every morning. "You'll never learn, will you, Cheryl? He's

forgotten you! Try to pick up the pieces and start again."

It wasn't till another week of hopeless dreams had gone by that I began to admit to myself that the unbelievable had really happened. Paul wasn't going to write. He'd forgotten all our promises.

I was sitting alone in the college cloakroom the next day at lunchtime. Alone, as usual, a huddled heap of miseries. When Lynne came in, I suppose she couldn't help feeling sorry for me. I mean, it wasn't so long before that we'd been the best of mates.

# Dreams

By the time I'd poured out all my miseries and sobbed on her shoulder that I hadn't meant to hurt Billy, she was offering me hankies and sympathy and telling me everything was going to be OK. I hadn't really told her how much Paul had meant to me, how much there had been between us. She thought I was just living on dreams. Maybe she wasn't so far wrong at that.

That night, alone in my room, there was no-one to see me take Paul's letters out of the box on my dressing-table, and tear them up, bit by bit, until they lay like tattered dreams littering my bedroom carpet.

I tidied all the mess away into my wastepaper basket and wished it was as easy to tidy away the mess of memories in my head.

But the warmth of my summer love was months behind me. Now there was only winter rain, thin and cold, tapping on my window . . .

I gazed at the remains of Paul's letters. My head told me I'd done the right thing — if only my heart would believe it . . .

"Cheryl! Are you there? Phone for you!" Mum yelled upstairs, breaking into my loneliness.

"Miss Sutton? Cheryl Sutton?" a woman's voice asked.

# Accident

"Yes." My voice trembled in reply.

"I'm Paul's mother. I've something to explain to you. I suppose it's too late, but, you see, since Paul's accident, everything's been so confusing."

"Pardon?" I gulped. It was all too much for me. I wasn't taking any of it in . . . just something about an accident. That bit stopped my heart dead.

"I'm sorry. I'm not explaining myself very well. I'm still at sixes and sevens . . . Paul was in an accident on his way back from holiday," Mrs Holt went on. "He was unconscious for weeks, and he kept saying your name. I'd no idea how to get in touch with you.

"Yesterday was the first time he was really able to explain about you, and he asked me to phone you. He's so worried that you'll think he's forgotten you. He's

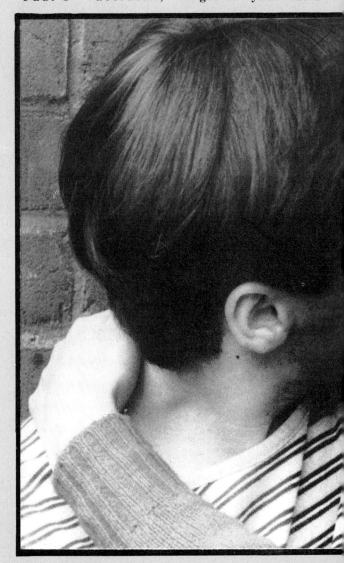

coming home next week, just in case you're still interested . . ."

Still interested! That was the understatement of the century! I'd thought he'd forgotten me! I'd thought it was all over. I'd thought . . .

"Yes! Oh, yes!" I managed to sob.

## Love

I don't really know what we said for the rest of that conversation. I know I asked a lot of questions and I know there were too many answers for my excited mind to take in. But, somehow, we arranged the visit I'd make, to see the boy I'd given up on, the boy who'd never stopped loving me as he'd promised to do.

Loneliness . . . it's part of the past now. Now there's love and laughter and friendship again where there was despair. And there's Paul, well again, holding me in his arms, repeating the promises he made to me so long ago, on a summer beach, in the sunshine of memories.

And as I curl into his kiss, into the happiness I thought I'd lost, I can't help thinking about something Paul once said when we first made all these promises — "Believe, and it comes true."

*The End*

## What's Cooking?

### COFFEE AND WALNUT BREAD

**Ingredients**
30 g wholemeal flour
¼ level teaspoonful salt
2 rounded teaspoonfuls baking powder
50 g butter
100 g caster suger
75 g walnuts (chopped)
3 rounded teaspoonfuls instant coffee powder
½ pint milk
1 beaten egg.

**Method**
1. Sieve the flour, salt and baking powder together, and then rub in the butter.
2. Mix in the sugar and nuts.
3. Dissolve the coffee in the milk and then add this and the egg to the mixture. Mix to a soft dough.
4. Place in a greased 900 g/2 lb. loaf tin and bake in the oven at Gas Mark 5 or 375 degrees for 1-1½ hours.
5. Serve cold, sliced and buttered.

### STUFFED PEPPERS

**Ingredients**
2 green peppers, halved lengthways and seeded
½ an onion, skinned and chopped
50 g bacon, chopped
38 g butter
2 tomatoes, skinned and sliced
50 g rice
Salt and pepper
2 level tablespoonfuls Cheddar cheese, grated
25 g fresh breadcrumbs
⅛ pint stock (from stock cube)

Preheat oven to 375 deg. F., Gas Mark 5.
Put the halved peppers in an ovenproof dish. Boil the rice and then drain. Lightly fry the onion and bacon in a little butter until golden brown. Add the tomatoes, cooked rice, seasoning and half the cheese. Mix the rest of the cheese with the breadcrumbs. Put the bacon stuffing into the peppers and sprinkle with the breadcrumb mixture. Pour the stock round the cases, top each with a knob of butter and cook just above the centre of the oven for 15-20 minutes.

# EVERY BODY'S TALKING!

*Did you realise that bodies speak louder than words? The way you stand, sit, hold a glass or lean against a wall all say something about you and they can make you fanciable or just plain forgettable!*
*Our special feature'll help you to make all the right moves!*

IMAGINE you're at a party. You don't really know a lot of people there, you've come on your own and you're feeling a bit shy, but you really want to enjoy yourself. *Blue Jeans'll* tell you the right and wrong ways to react.

Rule number one, when you walk into the room, don't immediately head for a chair in a quiet corner and perch on the edge of it with your knees together and your shoulders all hunched forward.

That'll simply tell anyone who's watching that you're really scared. Closed-in positions like that mean you're shutting out everything that's going on around you 'cos you don't know how to handle it. You're isolating yourself and your body is literally spelling out "leave me alone!"

If you stroll into the same room, smiling and looking round you, then lean casually against a wall and just watch what's going on — you may not actually feel the most confident person in the world, but you'll certainly look it!

Because you seem so relaxed and cheerful, other people — particularly fellas who're feeling a bit nervous themselves — will make a bee-line for you.

If you lean against the wall with one hand on your hip, a bored expression on your face, and your other hand casually stroking your hair — you're just asking for trouble! That's a real poser's position and any big-headed bloke who fancies boring someone to tears is going to sprint towards you as fast as he can! Two seconds later he'll have told you his life story and short of screaming for help or hitting him with a heavy object, you'll have problems getting rid of him!

If you sit back in a chair with your legs crossed above the knee, casually holding a glass and smiling round you interestedly, your chances of manoeuvring a manageable male to your side are a lot better! Just pick out the one you fancy in the crowd and keep smiling towards him. Sooner or later he'll get the message!

But if you come in, then sit down with your legs crossed at the ankles and your back very straight — guys'll probably steer clear of you 'cos you look far too prim and proper for them. They'll probably think you're a very serious type who's heavily into equal rights for snails!

If a guy asks you to dance and you get up very slowly, frowning and fussing with your dress — it'll probably be the *last* time he asks you!

But if you get up too fast, grab hold of him and giggle, that won't do you a lot of good, either! He'll just decide you're the over-anxious, clinging-vine type.

If you fancy him, it's much better to thank him and then get up as gracefully and unhurriedly as you can.

If you *don't* fancy him, he'll soon get the message if you just straighten your back and half-turn your head *away* from him, keeping your neck as rigid as possible.

BUT how can you tell if a guy fancies *you*? It's easy! Just follow the BJ guy-watching guide!

### THE SHY BABY!

If he's standing there, holding his drink, fidgeting with his feet and constantly looking or smiling in your direction, chances are he's liked what he's seen but he's a bit too shy to do anything about it.

If you like the look of *him*, just wander over — chatting to other people *briefly* on the way — and eventually arrive beside him. Make contact by doing something as simple as putting your hand on his arm and saying something corny like, ''Phew! It's hot in here!'' or ''D'you think you could possibly get me a refill?'' If he's willing, he'll promptly make physical contact with *you* — even if it's only by brushing his hand against yours as he takes your glass!

### PUPIL POWER

Not sure if it's you he's smiling at? Then we've got the eye-deal solution!

First: try to make eye contact with him then quickly lower your eyelids as if you're embarrassed at having been so forward.

Second: look back at him and smile again — then look away at someone else with a mournful expression on your face.

Third: take another look, smile, raise your eyebrows a bit as if you're trying to say, ''Who *are* all these people? I don't know a soul!''

If it *is* you he's after, it shouldn't be too long before he ambles over!

### MR SMOOTH

If he comes up to you, slings his arm confidently round your shoulders, grins down at you and delivers a line like, ''What's a nice girl like you doing in a place like this?'' — watch it! He fancies himself a lot more than he fancies you, and he's already handed out this patter to every other girl in the room!

Should you be daft enough to quite like the look of him anyway — put your hand on your hip, lean *away* from him a little and laugh quietly. Your body's now saying, ''I know your type, but you seem fairly harmless, so I'll hang around to see what you're going to come out with next!''

### THE BRUSH-OFF

If you'd rather he just left you alone, take the hand that's on your shoulders between thumb and middle finger (that's *your* thumb and middle finger, twit!) and remove it with a sort of brushing gesture as if it's something really nasty.

Raise one eyebrow at him (practise doing this in a mirror–it takes ages to get right, but it *does* work!) and then simply turn your back on him and talk to someone else. Your body has just said, ''Not a chance!''

See what we mean? You *can*, actually, say a whole lot of things — without ever opening your mouth! But it does take a lot of practice so just remember — no body's perfect!

# ONE GOOD TURN-OFF DESERVES ANOTHER!

**Jenny Nolan is fifteen. She's from Wrexham.**

''Well, let's face it, there's none of us perfect, but I'm as near as you're likely to find!

''No, seriously, I think there're things you like and dislike about anybody you meet, but generally speaking, I'd steer clear of guys with muscles or tattoos — I don't go for the he-man image at all!

''Puny males, queue here!''

**Sheila O'Sullivan is fourteen and comes from Enniskillen.**

''To me, there's nothing more revolting than a guy with chewed fingernails — and for some reason, the guys who have bitten nails are usually grubby as well! I mean, what could be worse than black, stubby, ragged nails! Ugh!''

**Greg Butchart's eighteen and he's a student from Edinburgh.**

''Girls who have to go everywhere in pairs really get on my nerves!

''I hate trying to chat up a girl who's giggling and whispering to her mate at the same time — and what about these females who even need each other's company to go off to the loo together at discos?

''It's as if they'd lose their way if they had to go by themselves! I know I'm not the only guy who's put off by this sort of 'Siamese twin' act!''

The guy you've fancied for ages is heading your way, then suddenly — AARGH! — you spot something about him that puts you off for life!

What would put *you* off somebody right away, we asked? The fellas had some pretty definite ideas, too . . .

**Fifteen-year-old Mo Richards is at school in Hastings.**

''I fancied this guy at school and I was really pleased when he asked me out. But when he turned up to meet me that night he was wearing a polyester suit! You know, the nasty, shiny sort! I can't bear that material!

''My baby brother has a pair of dungarees made out of that stuff and I can't even bear to touch it!

''Mind you, I needn't have worried about the polyester suit marking the end of a beautiful romance, 'cos he turned out to be really boring anyway, and I don't think he liked my red skintight jeans and red telephone-kiosk earrings. In fact, you could say we weren't very well *suited*!''

**Robert Wyman's an engineering student from Pontypridd.**

''A girl's hair's always the first thing I notice. Greasy hair or dandruff's a real turn-off, but I think the most off-putting thing of all is seeing dyed hair with the roots showing — yeugh!''

**Helen Low hails from Ipswich. She's seventeen.**

''Oh, string vests must be the foulest things ever invented! And why is it that the guys who wear them always seem to wear nylon shirts as well? Is it just so's nobody misses the tasteful cut of the vest? Honestly, how *could* they?

''Then again, another thing that's nearly as bad is the guy with the hairy chest who really fancies himself, so he wears his shirt open nearly to the waist and slings a medallion of some sort round his neck!''

**Stewart McEwan comes from Aberdeen. He's a student.**

''That's easy — black bras worn under light-coloured blouses and nicotine stains on fingers, though not necessarily in that order!

''I've yet to meet a guy who enjoys going out with a girl who smokes! It's like kissing an old ash-tray — and the memory lingers on the next day when your own hair and clothes still stink of stale smoke.

''My mate was sitting next to a girl at the disco last week and she accidentally burnt his jacket with a cigarette. It was the first time he'd worn that jacket and it'll probably be the last!''

# USE YOUR HEAD!

*Hairstyle by André Bernard.*

**Do you know the whole truth about hair? There're a lot of strange stories about it — and some of them are even correct! Test your knowledge now — you might be surprised!**

1. Your hair will grow faster if you get it trimmed regularly.
   True ☑   False ☐

2. You can buy hair lighteners which wash out afterwards if you don't like the colour.
   True ☑   False ☐

3. Redheads have less hair than blondes or brunettes.
   True ☐   False ☑

4. Lots of sport and exercise will make your hair grow faster.
   True ☐   False ☑

5. If you leave some conditioner on your hair after you've washed it, your locks will be softer and shinier.
   True ☐   False ☑

6. When something scares you, your hair stands on end.
   True ☑   False ☐

7. Your hair will break if you always wear it in a tight knot or plait.
   True ☐   False ☑

8. There's no point getting your hair cut if you want it to grow.
   True ☐   False ☑

9. Lemon juice can prevent blonde hair from darkening.
   True ☐   False ☑

10. You only need to use conditioner if your hair is dry.
    True ☐   False ☑

11. Hair is stretchy so it can take quite a bit of punishment.
    True ☐   False ☑

12. One hundred brush strokes every evening are needed to keep your hair glossy and healthy.
    True ☐   False ☑

13. If you're unwell your hair will look dull, too.
    True ☑   False ☐

14. Your fringe grows faster than the rest of your hair.
    True ☑   False ☐

**Now turn the page upside down to see if you need to brush up on hair!**

1. **False.** Hair grows from the roots beneath your scalp — so cutting has no affect on them. However, trimming can make your hair *seem* thicker by neatening off the straggly ends.

2. **False.** In order to lighten your hair, any product — no matter how "mild" — must contain bleach. And once your hair has had colour bleached out of it, it can't come back — unless you add dye on top! Temporary dark rinses *can* be washed out, though.

3. **True.** Blondes have most with an average head of 120,000 hairs. Brunettes are next with around 100,000, while redheads "only" have about 80,000. But that's still a lot!

4. **False.** It's certainly good for you, and will help you stay healthy — which in turn means you're more likely to have super-shiny hair. But nothing can change the speed your hair grows at.

5. **False.** If the instructions on your conditioner say it should be rinsed off, then leaving a film of it behind will actually dull your hair! What's more, it'll pick up dirt and dust faster. So, always rinse thoroughly with warm water.

6. **True.** Each hair has a tiny muscle attached to it underneath the skin. Like your other muscles, these tend to tense up when you get a shock. Normally, you'd just feel it as a sort of prickling sensation — but if you have very short hair you could actually see it stand up!

7. **True.** You risk your hair splitting around the hairline if you constantly scrape it back tightly. It's best to let it hang loose at least some of the time. Tying your hair with rubber bands can do a lot of damage, too — so stick to the covered kind.

8. **False.** There's every point! When you don't get it trimmed to get rid of ragged ends, splits just travel further up the hairs. So, unless you want to have six inches of fuzzy, messy ends, you'll finish up having to get a lot more chopped off!

9. **False.** There's no final rinse — or comb some splash to your final rinse. Add a does help to bring out fair highlights. but it doesn't make a big difference,

10. **False.** Conditioner improves all hair types — even greasy locks can be made silkier. The only people who don't need it are ones with very short hair.

11. **True — and false!** It does stretch when pulled, particularly when wet. If it didn't, you wouldn't even be able to comb it! But even so, too much tugging will weaken and break it, so treat it extra gently when it's at all damp.

12. **False.** Brushing too enthusiastically can actually split hair, and make a grease problem worse. The reason this was once popular was that in the past women didn't wash their hair as often as we do now — and lots of brushing was needed to remove the dirt!

13. **True.** The root of each hair is connected with your blood circulation and nervous system — so any illness affects your hair, too.

14. **False.** All your hair grows at the same rate — your fringe just seems to grow faster because it's right in front of your eyes!

46

**1** Toothache can be a killer — 'specially when it strikes on a Sunday, as it usually does! You can't get hold of a dentist, but you can ease the pain by chewing on a clove — check out the kitchen cupboards, as Mum should have some cloves handy.

And come Monday, make a dental appointment, then stick to your six-monthly check-ups!

**2** Something in your eye? No need to rub it till there's mascara streaming down your face — simply look up, down, to left and then to right a few times, and then blink repeatedly. That should shift it.

As a last resort, blow your nose. It works, honest!

**3** Everyone loves chips, but if you're ever cooking them at home take great care not to let the fat get too hot.

Should disaster ever strike and the fat catch fire, turn off the heat immediately, and cover the pan with a lid, fast, to stop the air getting to it. NEVER pour on water, which will only make things worse.

**4** Never tamper with anything electrical, 'specially faulty plugs or worn wires. But if you ever get an electric shock, touch some non-metal object right away — a wooden chair would do. Then sit down and breathe deeply, to try to relax.

**5** Minor burns are a common casualty in the kitchen. Ever scalded yourself with kettle steam, or been splashed by spitting fat? Well, immerse the burnt area in cold running water right away to ease the pain, before seeking medical help.

**6** Beware of nettles when you're out on a country ramble! But if you're unlucky and do get stung, look around for a clump of dock leaves. They're very common, and usually flourish alongside nettle patches — and if rubbed on a

# CRISIS~ What Crisis?

**Next time you find yourself in a sticky situation, don't just jump in with both feet — a bit of quick thinking can help you cope. We're here to show you how!**

sting, they take the pain away. No kidding!

**7** Ever turned your ankle and fallen off your high-heels? Then you'll know how painful a suspected sprain can be. But you can ease the agony by soaking your foot in warm water. If the swelling won't go down, and the pain persists, see a doctor.

**8** Sunbathing is a great way to relax, until it gets too much for you. If an overdose of sun makes you feel sick and faint all of a sudden, go indoors immediately, pull the curtains shut, and lie down in a cool, shady room.

**9** Choking on a mouthful of food can be very embarrassing, but it can also be dangerous. Don't try to cover it up by swallowing hard. Instead, cough into a napkin or hankie, till you remove the obstruction, then take a drink of water.

**10** Got a hair or a small bone stuck in your throat? Can't seem to shift it? Then chew and swallow a lump of dry bread. It might not be very tasty, but it works!

**11** Fainting fits are no joke — especially when you're in a crowded place, like at a pop concert

If it ever happens to you, as soon as you're able to, get into a sitting position and put your head down between your knees.

This'll get the blood flowing freely to your head again. Don't attempt to move, though, until you feel completely clear-headed again.

**12** Lost a prized possession? Don't give up hope of ever finding it again — report it lost to your nearest police station. If this fails, a cheap ad in your local newsagent's window or newspaper could come up trumps .

**13** Ever been lumbered with a hysterical child who won't stop screaming when you're babysitting? Try to attract his attention — a bright toy, a funny book, a daft trick or even some sweets should keep him happy. Just don't give up — and never be tempted to hit him!

**14** Late nights out can be great nights out, until you find yourself stranded, and miles from home. Whether you've lost your purse, missed the last bus or had a row with friends, you *must* get a message to your folks.

Find a phone and call them, or neighbours who can pass on the message. No matter what time of night it is, and whether you have to reverse the charges — so long as they know you're safe, no-one will mind the cost or the inconvenience.

If you can't get through, then call a local taxi firm (number from directory enquiries, dial 192) and say you'll pay when you reach your destination. It may not be cheap, but you can't put a price on your safety .

**15** Having a meal out? Faced with a dish that you hate, but can't refuse for fear of offending? Go ahead — refuse it. But politely. Far better to speak up now than feel sick all night!

The **Agony** Column

Tights are **VERY** mysterious

I mean, when you PUT them on...

they're tiny

BUT When You Take them **OFF**...

my Legs can't be THAT SHAPE, CAN THEY?

Continued on page 50

Continued from page 49

# HIDE and SECRETS

IT isn't just us girls who have secrets, you know. Boys can be sneaky too — trouble is, they're better at cover-ups than we are! So their secrets usually stay well hidden from prying eyes — until NOW!

Read on — if you dare! But be warned, it's not for those of you with delicate tums . . .

## Look At Me, I'm Lovely!

Now, this may come as something of a surprise to many of you, but boys actually do care about their appearance.

Difficult to believe, we know, when you catch sight of that scruffy twit in his oil-spattered dungarees and jumble sale sneakers. Ah, but that's your boyfriend, right? He's got used to you by now, and he's not trying any more! But just take a look around the available boys . . . and what d'you see . . . ?

## Bags Me First!

Just look at the Baggy Trousers Brigade! Reckon they're really trendy, right? Wrong! The boy in baggies isn't a devout follower of fashion — he's always worn 'em!

Reason? They conceal a pair of baggy legs beautifully!

*Denim jeans and jacket by Wrangler Check shirt by Wrangler Shoes from Freeman Hardy Willis*

## The Jean Machine!

Spot the tough guy always dressed in denim? He likes to think he looks like a Wild West Clint Eastwood type, straight out of a jeans ad!

He does, till you look closer . . . Aha! His secret's out! He's camouflaging a bulging tum! Because, you see, those hardy denims are the closest thing a flabby guy can get to a corset!

## People Like Polos!

Some boys seem to live in them! Polo neck jumpers, that is. The boy who favours these thinks they make him look smart and ritzy. And he *knows* they hide his unsightly bulging Adam's apple! Or worse — a grubby neck!

## The Padded Jacket!

M'mm, very suspicious — especially if he insists on keeping it on all the time. There can be only one reason for him to risk sweltering away in it under tropical conditions down at the disco . . . he's got something to hide!

Yes, this gear is a great cover-up for a Mr Universe physique — *before* he's taken a crash course in body-building.

Under those magnificent padded shoulders dangles the body of a seven-stone weakling! Shame!

But don't waste your sympathy on this boy, because he's smart, too. He knows that wearing a padded jacket is cheaper and less strenuous than buying a Bullworker!

**The Padded Jacket**
*Jeans and padded gilet by Wrangler Sweatshirt by Rebs Shoes from Dolcis*

*"Knit"-Wit*
*Jeans, sweater and T-shirt*
*by Pepe*
*Shoes from Dolcis*

# What A Knit-wit!

The typical boy who always sports natty patterned jumpers is not what he seems! No, he's not an ethnic freak into vegetarianism and saving the whale — he's just a big cissy with a bossy mum who threatens to stop his pocket money if he won't wear that pullover Auntie Gladys gave him for Christmas!

## ROOM FOR IMPROVEMENT!

If that little lot of shock secrets hasn't put you off fellas for life — there's worse to come! You really want an inside insight into what makes your boy tick? Then take a peek at his room — but only brave girls should try this one!

Pay no attention to the piles of clothes he's just tossed on the floor or the discarded, half-eaten cheese sarnies strewn around. Well, he's never tried to hide the fact he's an untidy twit and a mucky eater, has he?

Nope, you want his Secret Stashbox! Every boy has one. Invariably found under the bed. And inside you'll find a treasure trove (his opinion) of utter rubbish (any sensible person's opinion)!

Here're some of the things you're likely to find . . .

. . . A love-letter. Aaaaah! His first one. Also his only one.

It's from the girl next door, who is now tall, blonde and looks more like Debbie Harry than Debbie Harry does.

Wipe that anxious sweat off your brow. She wrote this letter to Loverboy when she was seven .

HIS SECRET . . . Either he's an incurable romantic, or he's madly in love with Deb-Next-Door, which would be a terrible pity as she's already got this six-foot bruiser of a boyfriend .

. . . A pair of six-inch soled platform boots. A relic of his days as a Gary Glitter fan.

HIS SECRET . . . He's still a Gary Glitter fan! Or else he's saving them for a confrontation with Deb's hulking boyfriend .

. . . His prize conker! With "Basher" lovingly inscribed on its side.

HIS SECRET . . . He has an overwhelming urge to be a world champion at anything. Conquering his classmates with conkers was the closest he ever got, though .

. . . A stack of unworn woolly vests!

HIS SECRET . . . He tells fibs! His mum buys him a new one every winter and he keeps telling her he's worn them out — but now *you* know the truth!

. . . Pimple potion! Tubes, jars, pots of ointment — enough to put Boots out of business!

HIS SECRET . . . He's terrified of breaking out in spots one day! Silly boy, he has no need to worry. If he keeps slapping on all that stuff, he won't have any skin left for spots to surface on!

So now you know the terrible truth! All fellas are far from perfect! Ah yes, but you've got to admit — they're still kinda cute with it!

# A Sad Song

*A special BJ story by Sue Papworth.*

I SEE you coming, balancing your cup of coffee through the crowds. You're coming over to me — and so I smile my cheer-you-up smile, a cheeky, cheerful grin.

"Hello, Paul! Pull up a chair. Have some sugar, have some salt, have some tomato ketchup, live a little!"

And despite yourself, you smile. I must be a good comedian.

"Hello, Katie. How's things?"

And so I tell you. Lots of cheerful things, things I've been doing, or might be doing, or might just think of doing. Look at me, Paul. I'm walking the tightrope, I'm juggling with pretty coloured ideas. Do you like them, Paul? Do they make you smile?

Yes, they make you smile. And when you go, you say, "It's been nice seeing you, Katie. You make life seem a bit brighter, somehow."

But, by the time you reach the door, your smile has faded. Mine has, too.

It's not always like that, though. There are different times, times when I don't play games to make you smile.

"I don't know what to do, Katie. I've tried to tell her, but I can't reach her, somehow. She looks at me blankly, and then talks of something else. But when *he* comes, her whole face changes."

I've sat opposite you whilst you've talked of her like that, sadness painting your face in weariness, and I've nodded and understood. Once, when things were very bad, I held your hand.

"You must stop trying, Paul," I said gently. "It'll only hurt you more to stay. You should go out and see other people, you should . . ."

But you were shaking your head. "No," you said. "I love her, Katie, and you can't just decide one day that you'll stop. It's not like that."

No, it's not like that.

And so I listen to you when you need to talk. And when talking isn't any help, I play the fool to make you smile.

"Thanks, Katie," you say to me, quite often. "You're a real friend."

And I'm glad to be your friend. Not happy, but glad.

Once, after a long, sad, grey afternoon when we walked together, and you talked of her endlessly, you smiled at last, a sad and crooked smile.

"It's like a song," you said, "the kind of song that you don't like, but it goes round and round in your head, always ending up with the same line — '*I love her: she loves him.*'" You smiled again, wryly. "It may not be a very good song, Katie, but I've got it on the brain."

I nodded and smiled, and we walked on together in the rain.

Yes, it is like a song, a sad little song that will never make the charts. Only you've got the words wrong.

It should go, *I love you: you love her: she loves him.*

*The End*

# Ever Sew Easy

*Add life to your wardrobe with
a few short cuts and simple stitches!*

## DOLLY MIXTURE!

This dolly bag would look great made out of half a metre of camouflage material — or you could use a piece of chamois leather or suede for a Red Indian-style bag.

Just cut a circular base about 20 cm in diameter, then cut a length of material long enough to fit round the base. (Allow about an extra 3 cm for a seam.) Turn a hem along the top and sew to make a channel through which a length of cord can be threaded. Sew along side seam, ending stitching just below channel for cord. With right sides together, attach the bag to the round base.

Thread through a length of cord for carrying, and decorate with some sewn-on fringing.

## KNICKER-BOCKER GLORY!

Bored with your baggy trousers? Try turning them into a pair of knickerbockers by cutting off the bottom of the legs to about 4 cm below the knee. Then turn the extra material into cuffs and add a couple of buttons for authenticity!

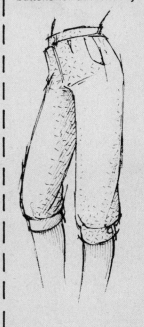

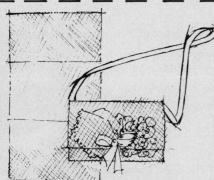

## NICE 'N' NETTY!

Going somewhere special and need a pretty handbag? Well, if you're only going to carry a few bits of make-up in your bag, net looks really pretty.

You can buy net relatively cheaply from most material stores. You'll need a piece about 45 cm by 30 cm and a couple of metres of satin or velvet ribbon.

Edge the net rectangle with ribbon then fold into an envelope shape and stitch two sides together, leaving the flap free. Use the remaining ribbon to make a carrying strap and a little tie so's you can close the bag.

## TWO-STEP STENCIL!

Pretty up a greying pair of plimsolls with fabric dye and a cardboard stencil. Just paint fabric dye on to your plimmie, leaving the areas covered by your choice of stencil white.

Hearts are an easy shape to cut out of cardboard, but if you're clever you could cut out more interesting stencils. If you don't want to leave the stencil shape white, you could carefully fill in the space with a different colour dye or even felt tip pens.

## TIERING ALONG!

Here's a tierful idea to gladden your wardrobe. If you have a long, mini-length T-shirt you could add rows of fringing, as illustrated.

Alternatively, if you have a large but shorter T-shirt you could add a couple of extra tiers of material to give this ruffled effect.

## ROMANTIC HEADLINES!

Bring out the gipsy in your soul by converting an ordinary head square into a stylish cover-up for scruffy hair.

Buy loads of sequins, tassels, gold and silver thread, and just cover the whole of the scarf with little bits of embroidery, adding sequins and shiny buttons here and there. Edge the scarf with tassels or threads of gold with sequins strung on the end.

## LOOP THE LOOP!

Why not tone up a plain, boring sweater with a few tassels?

Using a darning needle, sew large loops of wool on your jumper. Then snip the loops and tie them in a knot to keep them in place.

## JUNGLE FEVER!

Bring the excitement of the jungle to the front of your sweatshirt with an appliquéd native girl.

Just cut out shapes from felt or satin and stitch them on to your sweatshirt, to resemble a little girl. Add tassels swinging loosely for her skirt, and a little necklace of beads around her neck. You can make earrings by sewing on dangling threads with sequins on the ends to her head.

## CLINCH THE INCHES!

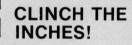

Str-e-t-c-h your wardrobe by giving a boring old shirt another lease of life.

Open out the shirt and pin some bias binding to the inside of the shirt in the position where you want the elastic to go. Sew this on, carefully leaving space to insert the elastic through the centre.

Thread through enough elastic to fit round your waist comfortably and stitch in place at the front edges of the shirt.

## SEW EASY!

Special parties and discos always make you feel you need something new and different to wear but if you're short of cash it's not always possible to afford anything.

Here's an idea for making a cheap tunic. All you need are a couple of metres of cheap cotton. Lay it out on the floor and cut to the shape illustrated. Make sure the square in the middle is big enough for your head to go through.

Trim the armholes, the neck and the hem with braid, then sew up the sides. Just add a belt and dive off to the disco!

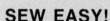

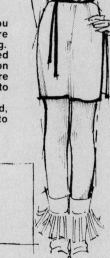

# VICTIMS OF

**Bullies rely on fear and silence — so if you're a victim, speak out!**

**B**EING bullied can be a nightmare experience. Once a bully has chosen you as his or her victim, it's very hard to fight back because bullies seem to thrive on draining all your confidence away.

Most girls, at some time or other, have had some experience of being pushed around by another person, or a gang. It can be just annoying, the feeling that you're being picked on or set up, or it can be horrifying, as it was in Jan's case.

Jan's sixteen now and seems very cheerful and friendly. But when she talks about what happened to her two years ago, it's difficult to imagine how she ever struggled through her own nightmare.

"It was a bad time," she told us. "Mum and I moved to the city after Dad left us, and I s'pose I was depressed at having to leave the country and all my friends, and not having Dad around.

"I was worried about Mum, too. She had so much on her plate that I didn't like to talk about *my* problems at the new school. It was terrible. I just didn't fit in at all.

"Maybe it was my fault, in a way. I didn't want to talk to anyone and even when one or two of the girls tried to be friendly I cut them off. I was lonely, homesick, and frightened.

"Well, this gang of kids, Tracy and Val and Linda and the others — I reckon they could sense how frightened I was. I'm little, too, still only five feet tall, even now. And when I was fourteen I was really skinny with it. They were all huge — or, at any rate, they looked huge to me, and a lot older in their ways. I was a bit of a country mouse.

## "THEY STARTED WALKING VERY CLOSE"

"They waited for me outside school one day at the end of the first week. I can't really explain how creepy it was—you know, about seven or eight big kids all standing there and then falling into step beside me.

"They were all smiling, asking me questions about where I came from, pretending to be friendly, and I thought maybe they were just trying to be nice to me.

"Then they started walking very close, pushing me around, and knocking into me, that sort of thing. I was walking to the bus stop, but somehow they *persuaded* me to give them my bus fare instead.

"That was just the start of it. Everywhere I looked at school the next day, I saw one of them grinning at me. They were waiting for the next payment. I didn't know what to do, or how to escape from it all. They were always there.

"If I couldn't come up with some money, they looked for something else. Tracy took my best pen, and Val made me give her some earrings Mum had bought me. Mind you, I'd've given them anything to get them to leave me alone.

"One day, when I'd nothing left to give, they all made a circle round me in an alleyway behind the school, and then pushed me from one to another. They emptied my bag out and left my books tattered and dirty.

"From then on, I started helping myself to money out of Mum's purse, just to pay them off.

"I couldn't tell her about it. She'd just started working full-time, and was always tired out.

"Then Mum began to notice that the money was missing, so I was only left one alternative. I stopped going to school.

"I used to leave in the morning, go round the back of the flats, and then let myself in with my key. Mum didn't realise. I was always home from school when she came home, anyway. In a way it was a relief, not having to face the gang. But it was hard making up stories about my day at school, and I was always scared that I'd get caught out.

## "I WAS TREMBLING ALL OVER"

"And, of course, eventually, I was! The Welfare Officer came up our stairs one day when I was creeping out to buy a bottle of milk. She took me straight round to school.

"All I can remember of that journey was me howling about not telling my mum, because she had enough to cope with. I was trembling all over when I had to face the headmistress. I thought I was in terrible trouble.

"It was a real eye-opener. I'd been scared rigid of the head-mistress, but she was just like a mum. She knew all about the problem at home and just seemed to want to help. I cried all over her and blurted out the whole story. It was what I should've done in the first place.

"Tracy and her mob were all split up and sent to different schools. I got a good talking to, but it was much gentler than I'd expected, and she did all the explaining to Mum.

"I was so relieved that I made a real effort to settle down and make friends, and look at me now! Still five foot nothing, but I reckon I could take on anything. Mrs Wilkes helped me get back the confidence I'd lost."

Sarah, the fifteen-year-old Manchester girl we spoke to, had a completely different story to tell.

"Bullying?" she asked. "You know, I didn't realise at first that I *was* being bullied. I thought I was having a great time, getting in with Gaz and Louis and the crowd at the café.

"Mum and Dad were really strict with me. It was all rules in our house. I practically had to give them a timetable whenever I went out! So I used to tell them I was going to the school drama club, or to choir practice, but I used to go down to the café in town and meet Gaz instead.

"He used to laugh about the way I lied to Mum and Dad. I really thought he was fantastic, living the way he did without any rules.

"We used to fly about on bikes, doing all sorts of crazy things. At least, Gaz thought up the things to do, and someone was chosen to do them. It was usually me.

"It was ages before I realised what was happening. All of them, Gaz and Louis and even the girls, Sue and Lynn and Sharon, saw that I was stupid enough to be pushed around, and they pushed.

"Then one night I dug my heels in. Gaz had this idea of breaking into the youth club. I was supposed to go through this window, but told him I wasn't having anything to do with something like that.

"But he wasn't going to let me back out — he threatened to tell my parents exactly what I'd been up to.

"I knew than I'd been conned and bullied and used — and now it was blackmail time. I thought Gaz cared, but I realised that he didn't care about me or anything else.

"So I did the hardest thing I've ever done in my life. I went home and told my mum and dad. Better to hear it from me, than from Gaz. They were stunned, really shaken. And I was in a terrible state. But there was no easy way out. I hated seeing how disappointed they were in me, and I had to put up with a load of new rules.

"It's easier, now. I actually go to that youth club, and I'm enjoying myself a lot more than I did at the café. Thank goodness I saw Gaz for what he was before it was too late!"

Chris was in her first job, as a clerk in an office, when her trouble started.

"I met Marie on the first day, and because she used to be at the same school I'd just left, we started talking. In fact, we became quite friendly. She was very popular in the offices, and, through her, I made a lot of new friends.

"Then I started going out with Mike, from Sales, and the atmosphere changed completely. Marie suddenly started avoiding me and all the girls glared at me, or sat at the next table to mine in the canteen and passed loud comments about me, and giggled.

"Then things started going wrong. I lost things from my desk, coffee was 'accidentally' spilled on my typing, and I'd get back from lunch to find a real mess on my desk.

"I didn't know what to do at first. I thought about talking it over with Mike, but I was sure it was something to do with me going out with him, so that didn't seem the right thing to do, somehow.

## "I'D HURT MARIE"

"So I tracked Marie down one lunchtime, and asked her about it. She knew nothing about the bullying at all and was really upset about it.

"She said she'd been out with Mike ages before, and he'd finished with her, and she was still very broken up about it.

"But that hadn't been the reason for her avoiding me. She'd been hurt because I'd not turned up for a cinema evening we'd arranged.

"I remembered then, that in the first week of going out with Mike I'd had that head-in-the-clouds feeling when nothing else mattered, and I'd completely forgotten I'd arranged to meet Marie.

"I told her how sorry I was, and somehow we made up our row. It had all been a misunderstanding and the other girls had got the wrong idea about why Marie was upset, and had decided to show that they could make life very difficult for me.

"Marie and I are the best of friends again, and it's just as well, really, because Mike finished with me soon after, and I needed her friendship very badly. She understood.

"I think talking to her that lunchtime, about the bullying was the best thing I ever did."

So there it is, three girls with different experiences of being pushed around, and different ways of coming through. But they all realised, one way or another, that the only way to stand up to bullying is to bring it out into the open. Because bullies, deep down, are cowards.

They trade in fear, and your silence.

So if you're being bullied or suspect that it's happening to someone you know, speak out — it's the only way to put an end to it once and for all.

# SCREEN & HEARD

Tune in to the BJ screen test and find out whether you're telly-pathic — or just telly-pathetic!

## From U.S. To You!

There're some terrific American programmes on the box just now. Let's see what you know about these Stateside stars!

1. Everyone loves to hate bad, old J.R. in Dallas — but do you know what his initials stand for?

2. This guy stars in which action-packed show?
3. Name the dishy actor who plays the part of Bo Duke in the Dukes of Hazzard.
4. Those terrific Baio brothers, Jimmy and Scott, star in two different TV shows — can you name them?
5. Which American city is the popular comedy series, Taxi, set in? Is it a) Los Angeles, b) Detroit, c) New York?
6. Robert Urich stars as which top Las Vegas detective?

## Picture This!

1. Can you name this bloke?
2. Which programme does he co-present?
3. In which sport did he gain a silver medal in the Olympic Games?

## Picture This!

1. What's this dishy fella's name?
2. Name the top TV series he stars in.
3. What's the name of the cheeky character he plays in the series?

## How Common!

What do the following groups of people have in common?

1. Dennis Waterman, Mike Berry, Penelope Keith.
2. Duncan Goodhew, Sebastian Coe, Steve Ovett.
3. Trevor McDonald, Richard Baker, Ronnie Barker.
4. David Vine, Reg Gutteridge, Peter O'Sullivan.
5. Colonel Wilma Deering, Twiki, Princess Ardala.
6. Tom Baker, Jon Pertwee, Peter Davison.

## TRUE OR FALSE?

We've been telling a few fibs here — so all you've got to do is answer true or false to each question.

1. Jim Davidson is a famous Cockney comedian.
2. The Muppets were created by Jim Henson and Frank Wizard.
3. Hurricane Higgins is a famous darts player.
4. Judith Haan is one of the presenters on Tomorrow's World.
5. Dusty Bin stars in top quiz show, Punchlines.
6. The comedy show M.A.S.H. is set in Korea.
7. Wendy Craig wrote and stars in Nanny.
8. Michael Parkinson is to host his own chat show for Australian TV.
9. Rowan Atkinson is usually on the Nine O'Clock News.
10. Legs and Co. introduce the Magic Of Dance.

## Spell-Tales!

We're really spelling it out for you! Take the first letter of the answer to each question and you'll be able to spell out the name of a top TV programme.

1. The Phantom Flan Flinger stars in this crazy show.
2. This kind of bear is a real favourite with Starsky and Hutch.
3. Greg's really on the road to success at BJ McKay.

4. Blue is this show's favourite colour!
5. Everyone wants to be this skater's perfect Cousin!
6. Hilda and Stan live down Coronation Street.
7. Anna was always in the news.
8. Miss Rantzen hosts That's Life.
9. This comedy show sounds like good, clean fun!
10. This Jim is great at fixing it.
11. Miss St Clair is Larry's favourite girl.
12. Muriel stars in Mixed Blessings.
13. Mr Edmonds doesn't want to swap his job!

14. Heavenly Nurses!
15. Comedian Sid, isn't very big.
16. Trevor Eve stars as top 'tec, Eddie.

# Picture This!

1. Can you name this good-looking actor?
2. What's his profession in the comedy show "Seconds Out"?
3. Name the programme in which he played Wolfie — leader of the Tooting Popular Front.

# At The Double!

Pre-pair yourself for our couple competition! All the stars below have to be paired up with their famous screen partner. It's not two difficult, honest!

# Words That Matter?!

Here're the names of some popular telly programmes. The only problem is that a word has been missed out in each one for you to fill in.

1. A Sharp Intake Of ------.
2. ---- You Were Here . . . ?
3. Ballyskillen ----- House.
4. Brendon -----.
5. Hill Street -----.
6. Holding The ----.

# I Say, I Say!

Just name the stars with these famous catch-phrases.

1. "I've started, so I'll finish."
2. "Nanu, nanu!"
3. "Ooooooh-Kaaaay!"
4. "Points make prizes."
5. "Walkies!"
6. "Fan Dabi Dozi!"

# ANSWERS

Score 1 point for each correct answer.

**From U.S. To You!**
1. John Ross. 2. California Fever. 3. John Schneider. 4. Soap and Happy Days. 5. (c). 6. Dan Tanna.

**Picture This**
1. Brian Jacks. 2. Ace Reports. 3. Judo.

**Picture This!**
1. Todd Carty. 2. Grange Hill. 3. Tucker Jenkins.

**How Common!**
1. They've all demonstrated their singing skills on 45's. 2. They're all Olympic gold medallists. 3. These fellas all wear spectacles. 4. They're all sports commentators. 5. These three star in Buck Rogers. 6. They've all played Dr Who.

**True Or False**
1. True. 2. False. It was Jim Henson and Frank Oz. 3. False. He's a snooker player. 4. True. 5. False. He stars in 3, 2, 1. 6. True. 7. True. 8. True. 9. False. He stars in Not The Nine O'Clock News. 10. False. Margot Fonteyn introduces the show.

**Spell-Tales!**
1. Tiswas. 2. Huggy. 3. Evigan. 4. Peter. 5. Robin. 6. Ogden. 7. Ford. 8. Esther. 9. Soap. 10. Savile. 11. Isla. 12. Odunte. 13. Noel. 14. Angels. 15. Little. 16. Shoestring.

**Picture This!**
1. Robert Lindsay. 2. A boxer. 3. Citizen Smith.

**At The Double!**
1. Brian Tilsley (Christopher Quinten) with 6. Gail Tilsley (Helen Worth) from Coronation Street. 2. Fran Shelley (Belinda Sinclair) with 7. James Shelley (Hywel Bennet) from Shelley. 3. Oliver Pride (Martin Jarvis) with 8. Sandy Pride (Diane Keene) from Rings On Their Fingers. 4. Jane Lucas (Maureen Lipman) with 5. Lawrence Lucas (Simon Williams) from Agony.

**Word's The Matter?**
1. Breath. 2. Wish. 3. Opera. 4. Chase. 5. Blues. 6. Fort.

**I Say, I Say!**
1. Magnus Magnusson. 2. Mork. 3. Lenny Henry. 4. Bruce Forsyth. 5. Barbara Woodhouse. 6. The Krankies.

If you scored 42 or over you really are switched on! There's nothing much you don't know about the box — in fact, you should go on Mastermind and choose telly programmes as your special subject!

If you scored 21-41 — you've got quite a good knowledge of the top programmes but you're definitely not square-eyed.

If you scored 0-20 — D'you know what a TV is? Well, it's that square object that sits in the corner of the lounge!

(Score an extra two points if you got them all right and discovered that the programme was "The Professionals.")

59

# I Thought It Was Wrong

## I knew Mum wouldn't approve of me going out  with boys — but then I met Don . . .

A READER'S TRUE EXPERIENCE

I COULDN'T bear the bad news to arrive by post, so, the day the O-level results came out, I walked up to school, to find out before Mum did.

The result sheets were pinned up on the walls round the hall, with a crowd of girls round each sheet. Some of the girls were jumping up and down and squealing, with happy looks on their faces. They were the lucky ones. Some of them were crying. I knew I'd be one of that group.

The trouble was, I just couldn't get it into anyone's head that I'd failed. Mum had been boasting to all the family that I would be staying on to do A–levels, because all my teachers said I was going to do well. I'd expected to do well, myself, up until a week or so before the exams.

I walked from group to group, confirming what I'd already known, still unable to control that sinking feeling in my stomach. Some of my friends must have seen my rotten results, too, because one or two of them gave me really pitying looks, afraid to say anything in case I burst into tears.

I'd failed everything except art, the last exam, the exam I took on the morning I got that private reply from the magazine I'd written to.

I didn't know how I was going to explain to Mum. I'd never dared tell her about the state I was in during those exam weeks. I couldn't talk to her about that sort of thing.

Mum had brought me up really strictly. She encouraged me to do well at school. That was something she understood, school work. She's older than most mums, and Dad had been even older than her.

He'd died when I was ten, and since then Mum'd kept me going with my schoolwork by telling me, "Your father would've been proud to see you doing so well, Emma, if only he'd lived to see this day!" Whenever she said that, it gave me a sense of pride, yet it was as if my life was being lived to please a ghost.

Mum missed Dad terribly, and used my hard work and intelligence to fill the gap he'd left.

## DISAPPROVING

The trouble was, she never understood that I was a girl as well, a girl with things to live for other than

60

exams and college, one day. She kept a very tight rein on me, keeping me at home with her, disapproving of the way my friends at school "carried on," and believing that boys were just a waste of time.

She'd been a librarian, well over thirty when she married Dad, and had led a very sheltered life. I could never talk to her about the personal things that bothered me.

Boys bothered me. But the thought of asking Mum about them turned my blood cold. She'd be more embarrassed than me.

I'd never taken biology at school and there was so much I didn't know. I felt left out when the other girls talked about what they'd been doing. I wasn't just left out, I was terrified when I picked up bits and pieces of what they talked about.

It sounded awful, just as Mum had said it was, not in words, but in the look on her face whenever there was anything like that on television. She always turned it off, tutting and clucking.

But I wanted to be like the other girls, so I pretended I knew as much as they did. They all thought I was a bit "odd." I didn't want them to know that I was ignorant as well, as far as some things were concerned.

## KIND

My big night out was a night-school class in art at the local college. Art was my best subject, and Mum encouraged me to go to the classes which dealt with more advanced work than at school.

I met Don there. I didn't take much notice of him at first, because I was too busy painting, but I knew his name, and I liked the way he'd come over to look at what I was doing, and try to say something complimentary about it. He was very kind and I noticed what lovely eyes he had, brown and melting, but crinkling into laughter so easily. We got into the habit of strolling home together.

I don't know why he bothered with me. I'm not bad-looking, but I don't wear very fashionable clothes and I'm not exactly relaxed with boys. I was with Don, though. I was relaxed enough to let him kiss me goodnight a couple of times, on those warm Spring nights, as we walked through the empty park. And suddenly, I wasn't thinking about much more than the

gentleness of his lips on mine, and the strange, soft feeling I had whenever he was close.

I tried to put him out of my mind, but on the last night of the art classes I was heartbroken that I'd probably never see him again. I wasn't given enough freedom to go out to discos, or to the pictures, unless it was an animal film that Mum wanted to see. Then she came with me.

So, on that last night, I tried to smother the surging tears and the bitter sadness I felt, and when Don took me in his arms for one goodnight kiss, I let myself

go completely. At least that's what it felt like when I came to my senses and broke away from him in panic.

I couldn't believe that it was me, doing things like that. I ran, sobbing, away from him, ignoring his shouting for me to come back and asking what was the matter. I was too ashamed to look at him, let alone reply.

I was just glad that he didn't know where I lived and couldn't follow me home. We'd always parted at the edge of the park. Mum would've had a fit if she'd

seen me coming home with a boy.

## TERRIFIED

The panic I felt at that moment didn't go away. It haunted me in dreams and nightmares, all the guilt I felt at deceiving Mum and behaving so badly. My exams were due to start, and I couldn't concentrate on anything, especially when I really started getting terrified — I was late.

I'd been late before, in fact, I wasn't very regular at all, but this time I thought I knew why.

I remember the white-cold

fear that shook my hand right through the first exam. I knew I was going to fail. I couldn't remember anything, I couldn't think about anything but trying to explain to Mum that I was pregnant.

I did the only thing I could in the end and wrote to one of those problem pages in a magazine, explaining everything, what I'd done, why I was terrified. I told them it was urgent and hoped they'd reply straight away.

I couldn't ask anyone else. There was no-one I could talk to about it,

certainly not one of the other girls. They'd laugh, and it would be all over the school in no time. "You'd never believe this, but. . ." I could just imagine it.

## FREEDOM

So I did my exams and tried to fill the lined white paper with words, any words, while I thought out the words I'd choose to tell Mum. I knew I was writing rubbish. I was just getting through from day to day until the reply came.

I managed to sneak that letter in without Mum seeing it, locking myself in the bathroom to read it.

"Dear Emma," it said. "You are worrying unnecessarily. There is no possible way that you could be pregnant from doing what you describe. There is nothing unnatural or strange about it, and most girls have had similar experiences at your age. Please don't feel guilty about such an innocent and loving moment in your life. Do try to talk to your mother."

I memorised every word. Then I tore the letter up, flushed it down the toilet, and went to school to take my art exam.

I suppose the letter changed my way of looking at things. I wanted to know all about the gentler side of loving, not being terrified all the time. So, in the long summer holidays I'd tried to read as many books as I could, and once, I asked Mum, "What was it like, being in love with Dad?" and slowly, she managed to tell me, although I could see it was very difficult for her.

I'd been asking her, too, as carefully as I could, about more freedom. And I'd mentioned Don's name.

I'd had to do that, because I knew I had this to face, the day I had to tell her that I'd failed my exams because I was frightened after a boy kissed and touched me in the park. I had to tell her that I'd been frightened of knowing so little about real life.

I'd spent my time with my head in books and I was painfully ignorant. I just had to tell her the whole story, no matter how much it hurt. I could resit the exams in November, and I'd probably pass.

But this talk with Mum, I had to pass that, first go. I had to get through to her. I just wiped away the odd tear, and headed for home to shatter her dreams. And to try to build something new, too.

# PLAY IT AGAIN, SAM

HERE WE GO AGAIN, WALKIES IN THE PARK AND ALL THAT... SNIFF, SNIFF...

NOT THAT I DON'T LIKE THE PARK, MIND YOU. BUT EVERY WEEK IT'S THE SAME—TWICE ROUND THE PATH...

...A QUICK DRINK AND, OH, LOOK— DUCKS! OH, DRAT! NOT ALLOWED TO CHASE THE DUCKS. ALMOST FORGOT.

THEN IT'S THE OLD STICK-CHASING BIT. HURRY UP AND THROW IT, YOU SILLY GIRL. CAN'T STAND AROUND HERE ALL DAY!

OH-OH, HERE'S THE BENCH. SUPPOSE WE'LL GET THE OLD BROKEN-HEARTED ROUTINE NOW...

TELLS ME ALL HER TROUBLES, DOES SUSIE. AND SHE SEEMS TO HAVE PLENTY OF THEM!

OH, SAM, WHAT AM I GOING TO DO? JOHN'S FOUND SOMEONE ELSE.

Continued on page 64 63

Continued from page 63

**THE END**

Who says long hair's boring?
Before you give it the chop, try
these super plaited styles —
Heidi never looked so sophisticated!

## Centre Plaiting

**1** With all these styles, for the best result, get your hairdresser to do it first and watch carefully. With practice (and perhaps a little bit of help from a friend!) you should be able to copy it afterwards.

For this one, start making a plait at the centre top of your head and take it right down the back. As you go, pull a small section of hair in from the side of your head to join with the outer section of the plait. At the same time, move a piece of hair from the middle of the plait to the inside section, to keep it even.

Tie it at the end with a covered elastic band and finish off with a clip.

65

# Bride's Plait

**2** Although this lovely, feminine style is particularly popular with young brides, it'd be equally stunning for a special party or dance.

To make it, start with a small plait just above one temple. Twist it inwards and, joining two strands together and picking up a new one with each crossover, move round to the back in that way.

Hold it at the nape of your neck with a covered elastic band while you do the same at the other side. Then join the two tails together with an elastic band and curl them under. Cover the band with a flowered clasp or comb.

# Surprise Plait

**4** The top section of hair is plaited from above your ear at one side, diagonally down to the opposite shoulder. Looks very exotic!

Like the other close-to-the-head plaits, you make it as for a normal one, but each time, bring an extra piece of hair from the side into the section you're moving over to the middle, and move a little of the middle section over to the inside.

Take care not to twist the plait — and finish it off with a flower tucked into a covered elastic band.

# La Hoop!

**5** Here the hair is parted right down the middle, and two close-to-the-head plaits made from your temples round to the nape of your neck, pulling extra hair in as described before.

Join the plaits up at the base and secure with a flower-covered elastic band. Or, for a neater look, curl the tails up and pin them neatly in with the plaits.

# Take It Back!

**3** Tie back the middle section of your hair. Start plaiting the side section just above your temple, pulling in extra hair from the crown (to hold the plait close to your head) for about two inches, then continuing it as a normal plait.
Do the same at the other side then join the two plaits together at the back with a covered elastic band.

# Crowning Glory

**6** Make a horizontal parting across the crown of your head from ear to ear, and tie your hair back out of the way. Starting above one ear, make a plait along the line of the parting, joining a side piece into the middle and pulling an extra section of hair into the side, as before, till you end at the other ear.

You could leave it at that — a plaited headband! Or, as in the pic, add two thin plaits at the side, starting them from just below the crown plait.

*Blue Jeans Beauty*

*Thanks to Nicola of the Clifford Stafford Hair Salon in London for these terrific styles.*

# DIAMONDS ARE A GIRL'S BEST FRIEND

## And you'll certainly sparkle in this super sweater!

**Materials.** —
Jaeger Mohair-Spun

| | | | | | |
|---|---|---|---|---|---|
| Light (L) | 15 | 15 | 16 | 16 | 25 g. balls. |
| Contrast (C) | 1 | 1 | 1 | 1 | 25 g. ball. |

Pair needles each Nos. 5 (5½ mm) and 7 (4½ mm).

Set of four No. 7 (4½ mm) needles.

**Measurements.** —

| | | | | |
|---|---|---|---|---|
| To fit bust | 81 | 86 | 91 | 97 cm |
| | 32 | 34 | 36 | 38 ins. |
| Length from | 62 | 63 | 65 | 66 cm |
| Shoulder approx. | 24½ | 25 | 25½ | 26 ins. |
| Sleeve seam | 43 | 43 | 43 | 43 cm |
| | 17 | 17 | 17 | 17 ins. |

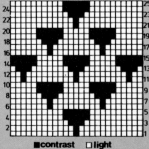

■contrast ☐light

**Tension.** — 8 sts and 10½ rows to 5 cm *(2 ins)* over st-st. on No. 5 (5½ mm) needles.

**Abbreviations.** — K — knit; P — purl; sts — stitches; st. st. — stocking-stitch; inc — increase, increasing; dec — decrease, decreasing) beg — beginning; alt — alternate; rep — repeat; cm — centimetres; ins — inches.

## FRONT

Using No. 7 (4½ mm) needles and L, cast on 68 (72, 76, 80) sts.

**1st row.** — K3, (P2, K2) to last st, K1.

**2nd row.** — K1, (P2, K2) to last 3 sts, P2, K1.

Rep these 2 rows for 10 cm *(4 ins)*, ending after a 2nd row and inc 4 sts evenly on last row. 72 (76, 80, 84) sts.

Change to No. 5 (5½ mm) needles and beg K row work in st.st. for 10 rows.

Continue in st.st. working from chart thus:

**1st row.** — 43 (45, 47, 49) L, work 1st row from chart, 4 (6, 8, 10) L.

**2nd row.** — 4 (6, 8, 10) L, work 2nd row from chart, 43 (45, 47, 49) L.

**3rd to 25th rows.** — Rep 1st and 2nd rows 11 times, then 1st row again working 3rd to 25th rows of chart.

Work 5 rows in L.

**Next row.** — As 2nd but working 1st row from chart.

**Next row.** — As 1st but working 2nd row from chart.

**Next 23 rows.** — Rep last 2 rows 11 times, then 1st of these rows again working 3rd to 25th rows of chart.

Work 5 rows in L.

**Next row.** — 33 (35, 37, 39) L, work 1st row from chart, 14 (16, 18, 20) L.

**Next row.** — 14 (16, 18, 20) L, work 2nd row from chart, 33 (35, 37, 39) L.

Continue as on last 2 rows working rows 3 to 11 from chart at the same time shaping armholes by casting off 3 (4, 5, 6) sts at beg of next 2 rows. Then dec 1 st at each end of next 3 rows, then on the 2 following K rows. 56 (58, 60, 62) sts.**

Keeping chart correct and noting that when 25th row has been worked, remainder of front will be worked in L, continue until armhole measures 10 (11, 11, 13) cm, *4 (4½, 4½, 5) ins*, ending after a P row.

Shape neck thus:

**Next row.** — K21 (21, 22, 22), turn. Continue on this group.

Dec 1 st at neck edge on next 4 rows. 17 (17, 18, 18) sts.

Work straight until armhole measures 18 (19, 20, 21) cm, 7 (7½, 8, 8½) ins, ending at armhole edge.

Shape shoulder by casting off 6 sts at beg of next and following alt row. Work 1 row. Cast off.

With right side facing slip next 14 (16, 16, 18) sts on a spare needle. Rejoin yarn(s) and K 1 row. Complete as first half.

## BACK

Work as front to**
Work straight to match front until back measures same as front to shoulder shaping.

Shape shoulders by casting off 6 sts at beg of next 4 rows, then 5 (5, 6, 6) sts at beg of next 2 rows. Slip final 22 (24, 24, 26) sts on a spare needle.

## SLEEVES

Using No. 7 (4½ mm) needles and L, cast on 32 (32, 36, 36) sts.

Work in rib as on welt for 10 cm (4 ins), ending after a 2nd row and inc 1 (5, 5, 9) sts evenly on last row. 33 (37, 41, 45) sts.

Change to No. 5 (5½ mm) needles and st.st. shaping sleeve by inc 1 st at each end of 9th row, then on every following 6th row until there are 43 (47, 51, 55) sts. Work 3 rows.

**Next row.** — K9 (11, 13, 15) L, work 1st row from chart, K9 (11, 13, 15).

Continue working rows 1 to 25 from chart as placed on last row at same time shaping sleeve as before by inc 1 st at each end of 2nd row following, then on every following 6th row until there are 51 (55, 59, 63) sts.

Continue in L only until sleeve measures 43 cm (17 ins), ending after a P row.

Shape top by casting off 3 (4, 5, 6) sts at beg of next 2 rows.

Dec 1 st at each end of every K row until 23 sts remain, then on every row until 15 sts remain. Cast off.

## NECKBAND

First join shoulders. Using set of No. 7 (4½ mm) needles and L, right side facing, K up 76 (80, 88, 92) sts evenly round neck including sts on spare needles. Work in rounds of K2, P2 rib for 9 cm (3½ ins). Cast off loosely in rib.

## TO MAKE UP

Press following pressing instructions, omitting ribbing. Join side and sleeve seams. Sew in sleeves. Fold neckband in half to wrong side and hem in position. Press seams.

# Tell Him I'm Sorry...

A Short Story by Sue Papworth.

**M**OIRA looked at Angie in disbelief. "Why on earth do you want to bother with *him*? He's about as much fun as a wet week in Blackpool!"

"Oh, he's not! He's dreamy — I think he's got a secret in his past!" said Angie, rummaging in her bag for her comb. "Still waters run deep, you know!"

"I *said* he was wet," giggled Moira.

They were talking about Ian Brown, the good-looking but terribly quiet boy in the next office. And they were ignoring me, as usual. I suppose neither of those things was surprising.

He'd had all the girls in the place in a buzz for ages after he arrived, with his dark hair and tanned face, and I was shy and quiet and didn't chatter and nudge and giggle like the others did.

Ian wasn't just good-looking, either, he was *nice*. He always smiled and said hello, and held the door open for you.

Angie and Moira went on giggling and talking, but I turned back to my typewriter with a sigh and started pounding away at another pile of work. What's the use of thinking . . .

Then, that weekend, I saw the message in the paper, buried away among the small ads.

*Ian, where are you? Will somebody please, please tell Ian Brown that I'm sorry and I love him and I miss him and I*

want him back — Jerry.

I blinked. So, he **did** have a secret in his past! I read it again, wondering who Jerry was, and if she was terribly pretty, and why they d quarrelled, and if he missed her terribly much. But what if he hadn't seen the message? Maybe I should tell him.

On Monday, I watched Ian, and thought about the message. He smiled at people, but his eyes were sad. And I knew why . . .

At lunchtime, I followed him — he sat in a quiet café over a sandwich and coffee, looking lonely and lost. I sat there and thought about Jerry. Was she sitting all alone and sad, too? Or was she hiding away, crying her heart out? I would have been.

I imagined him seeing the message, and the look on his face, and then both of them running into each other's arms . . .

I felt all soft and sad, and sort of responsible, somehow. I had to do something, but I just didn't know how to walk up to a boy in a café and start talking to him — never mind discussing his love life!

By the time I'd made up my mind to do it, he'd left the café. I hurried after him but he'd reached the office door before I could catch up with him. I just smiled as he held the door for me.

After work, I dashed out of the office ahead of the others, ignoring Moira and Angie's amazed stares. Ian was in front of me, and I saw him go into the same cafe.

Taking a deep breath, I followed him in, and carried my cup of coffee over to his table.

"Hello, Ian," I said shyly. "I've got something to show you. Do you mind if I join you?"

He looked surprised, but smiled, and nodded.

"Yes, Carol, of course. What is it?"

I rummaged in my bag, and brought out the folded piece of paper. "It's a message for you," I said.

He took it from me, and began to read. I watched his frown of concentration, and the changing expression in his soft brown eyes.

"Do phone her," I said, impulsively, putting my hand on his. "You've been looking so unhappy."

He looked up at me, and smiled, and I thought wistfully, *lucky, lucky Jerry.*

But then he put down the paper, and laid his other hand over mine.

"How nice you are," he said. "I always thought you were nicer than the others. You notice things about people, and you care."

"But . . ." I said. "There's Jerry . . ."

"There must be loads of Ian Browns," he said. "I hope he finds her, if she's half as nice as you."

"You mean it's not . . .?"

"No. Not me. But, thank you."

"But you seemed so lost, so lonely, that I thought . . ."

"Yes, I'm lonely. Or I was. It's easy to be, if you're shy."

*Shy!* I'd never even thought that good-looking, gorgeous people like Ian could be shy . . .

"I can't talk to girls who just giggle," he went on, "like Angie and Moira. They embarrass me. But you're different."

He grinned. "I've been trying to pluck up courage to talk to you for ages. You're braver than I am."

"Brave!" I said. "Me! I was scared stiff."

And suddenly, everything was all right. In fact, it was marvellous!

"Thank you, Jerry," I thought. "And I hope you find your Ian, too."

69

# BEHIND THE SCENES

These record makers tell us about the ups and downs of the music business.

### Rita Ray, Darts

"Dressing-rooms are something you've got to learn to live with in the music business. Some theatres have nice, large rooms, but in most places it's like trying to get dressed in a dustbin!

"You bump into everything and everyone, and visitors and Press people are all trying to talk at once while you leap around standing on everyone's toes!"

### Andy Summers, The Police

"Troubles in the music business usually arise whenever money is mentioned.

"Too many people assume that most popular groups are rolling in cash which is often not the case.

"New bands sometimes get advances from their record company — but it's only a loan and as soon as they begin to make money they have to pay most of it back!

"You also have to consider the cash they must pay out on stage clothes, travelling and musical equipment."

### Feargal Sharkey, The Undertones

"To me, the best bit about being a pop star is all the recording work.

"It's always very demanding and exciting and it's terrific to hear the songs you've written when they're the finished product.

"But it's not all fun 'cos studio time is extremely expensive so you've got to work fast. Albums can take anything from a few weeks to months to make, depending on what you're trying to do.

"To give you an example, our album cost about £20,000 to make, whereas Fleetwood Mac spent over a million dollars!"

### Cliff Richard

"Working on television is important to any pop star and this can be very hard work — but also lots of fun.

"An appearance on a show like 'Top Of The Pops' means that millions of people can not only hear your new song but also take a good look at you, too!

"Obviously, you've got to look your very best 'cos this can really boost your record sales. That cancels out any late-night festivities for a week before the programme — otherwise all they'll see is a mass of wrinkles and a pair of bleary eyes!

"It's not all fun and games in the music world, you know!"

### Dave Bartram, Showaddywaddy

"For our style of music, fashion is very important and we've always to look our very best.

"Our type of gear gives the kids something to identify with and they can also recognise the type of music that we play by it. I mean, our drape suits show that we love rock 'n' roll.

"Sometimes, I'd just like to turn up to a concert in my old, comfy jeans and a T-shirt, but I know I can't 'cos our fans would be very disappointed. In the music business you just can't let the public down."

70

## Sheena Easton

"I haven't been involved in the pop world for very long but I've already learned to appreciate the importance of good photography.

"It's extremely boring and nerve-racking spending the whole day in the studio under very hot lights and hearing the endless click, click of the cameras.

"But you have to realise that the shots will be extremely useful for your career 'cos they'll be printed in magazines and newspapers and can also be used for album covers."

## Jimmy Pursey

"Live concerts are always exciting but you never know quite what to expect.

"Is the audience going to warm to your music or are they going to be hostile and aggressive? These are risks you've got to take.

"The real thrill is being able to reach people with your music when you can't do it properly through records.

"Mind you, there's lots of preparation to be done for concerts. Equipment has to be set up and tested, sound checks made and lighting arranged. They have their advantages, though, 'cos all that work plus leaping around on stage for a couple of hours is a great way of losing some weight!"

## Paul Weller, The Jam

"I don't think many people outside the pop business fully appreciate the travelling we musicians have to do.

"Touring in Britain is hard enough, as your van'll probably break down at least half a dozen times!

"Going abroad is even worse 'cos sometimes the language barrier can be really frustrating and you end up in the wrong concert hall, in front of the wrong audience in the wrong town!"

## Bob Geldof, The Boomtown Rats

"Working abroad can be really exciting and tough.

"The travelling is the most tiring aspect of it, but playing to new audiences is such fun it seems to give you extra energy.

"In America it's no use doing only one tour. The place is so big that they'll have forgotten who you are in Washington by the time you've arrived in L.A.!

"I never get the chance to do any sight-seeing on my travels — it's just one endless stream of concert halls and hotel rooms. But that's what the pop business is all about!"

## Paul Di'Anno, Iron Maiden

"Trying to get a decent square meal every day is always a problem in the pop world.

"Groups tend to eat at odd hours of the day. Have you tried finding a restaurant that's open at four o'clock in the morning?!

"So now you know why most pop stars are slim. It's not vanity — it's just the way things work out!"

# KNOT LIKELY!

**Macramé is so easy to do, you'll soon have this cute owl all tied up!**

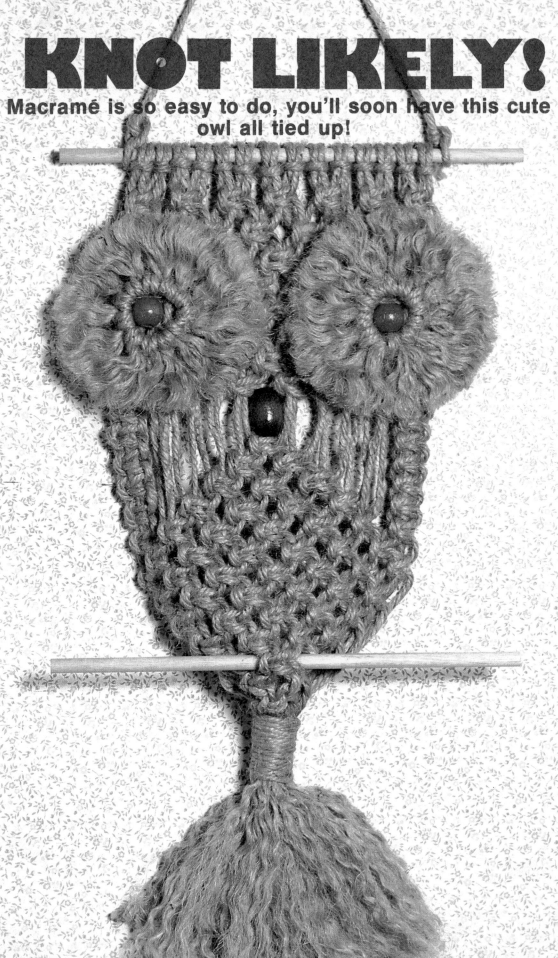

## IMPORTANT:

This is a very simple pattern, but if it's the first time you've tried macrame, it's a good idea to practise setting on cords and working the flat knot before you start.

### Setting On Cords

Take each cord, fold it in half, pass the loops forward over the rod and down behind it as in fig. 1a. Push the ends through the loop and pull tight as in fig. 1b. This is known as a Lark's Head knot.

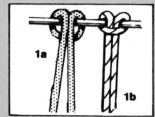

### The Flat Knot

A flat knot is formed with groups of four cords. It is tied using the outside two cords only. The two middle threads form a centre or core and should be pulled taut again as each knot is completed. This helps to keep the tension even.

### Working Half the Knot

Take the left-hand cord A and place it over the two centre threads and under B (as in fig. 2a).

Take right hand cord B, pass it behind centre cords and up through the loop formed by A. Pull threads A and B sideways to tighten and complete the half knot (Fig 2b).

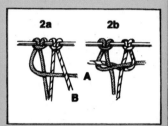

### Completing the Knot

Take cord A (now at the right-hand side of the work) across the front of the two centre cords and under cord B as in fig. 2c.

Pass cord B behind the centre cords and up through the loop made by cord A (fig. 2d).

Pull cords A and B sideways to tighten and complete the whole flat knot.

### Diamond Pattern of Flat Knots

Using blocks of four cords, work a row of flat knots from left to right.

Before working the second row, re-group the cords (see fig. 2e). Leave two spare cords at each end of the row and divide the remaining cords into groups of four (two cords from each knot on the previous row).

Work a second row of flat knots using the new groups of four cords, ignoring the two spare cords.

Re-group cords into blocks of four, including the two spare cords once again, and repeat first row.

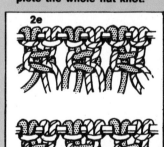

### Flat Cord

This is made by repeating the complete flat knot (Figs. 2a, 2b, 2c and 2d) on the same threads.

### Sinnet

This is another name for a narrow length of knotting such as a flat cord. (3a).

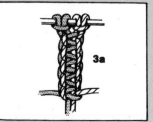

### Abbreviations

FK — flat knot, R — right, L — left, RHS — right-hand side, LHS — left-hand side.

## YOU'LL NEED

*Approx. 25 metres 4-ply jute*
*1 large oval bead*
*2 medium round beads*
*2 pieces of dowel rod 30 cm long*
*OR 2 lengths of driftwood*
*Needle and thread*

## METHOD

Cut 14 lengths of cord each 150 cms long.
Fold each cord in half and set on to a dowel rod with lark's head knots.
Number cords from 1-28.
Cords are *always* numbered from left to right, and sequence never changes even when the cords switch places.

1. Work 1 row FK on threads 1-28.
2. Work 1 row FK on threads 3-26.
3. As row 1.
4. As row 2.
5. Work 1 row FK on threads 5-24.
6. Work 1 row FK on threads 7-22.
7. Work 1 row FK on threads 9-20.
8. Work 1 row FK on threads 11-18.
9. Slip large oval bead on to threads 14-15, and push to top.
10. Tie one FK on threads 13-16, immediately below bead.
11. Work 1 row FK on threads 11-18.
12. Work 1 row FK on threads 9-20.
13. Work 1 row FK on threads 7-22.
14. Work 1 row FK on threads 5-24.
15. Work sinnets of 10 FK on threads 1-4 and 25-28.
16. Work 1 row FK on threads 3-26.
17. Work 1 row FK on threads 1-28.
18. Work 1 row FK on threads 3-26.
19. Work 1 row FK on threads 5-24.
20. Work 1 row FK on threads 7-22.
21. Work 1 row FK on threads 9-20.
22. Work 1 row FK on threads 11-18.
23. Work 1 FK on threads 13-16.
24. Gather threads together and, using 100-cm length of cord, wrap a 4-cm length immediately below last FK.
25. Trim the ends of the threads back to 15 cms. Unravel and "fray" ends of threads to form tail.
26. Push a length of dowel rod or driftwood through the work as a perch.

## WRAPPING

Make a loop at end A, then holding carefully in place, wrap cord tightly round all cords, including loop, working upwards. Pass end B through loop then pull end A until loop is secured under wrapping. Trim ends A and B.

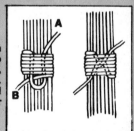

## TO MAKE EYES

Using lengths trimmed from tail, cut 20 x 20 cm lengths.
Set 10 lengths on to another length of cord (see Fig 4a). Tie ends of the cord together and pull tightly to form a circle.
Fray the ends of cord until fluffy.
Trim to 4 cms (see Fig 4b).
Repeat for other eye.
Sew a round bead into the centre of each eye. Position eyes on body as shown.

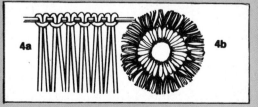

## TO FINISH

Tie a length of cord on to top dowel rod to act as a hanger.

A Special BJ Story
by Sue Papworth

# The Magic Of Love...

IN the twilight shadows, moths with shimmering wings fluttered across the path on the scented summer breeze. I waited by the rowan tree where the honeysuckle twined, listening to the soft country sounds around me.

I gazed over the meadows to the forest, lost in thought — until I heard him whisper my name: "Janet." I felt his gentle touch on my hair, and he swept me, laughing, into his arms. I looked up into his blue eyes. They smiled beneath the thick sweep of fair hair. Tam: my own Tam Linn. Before the honeysuckle faded, I would be his wife.

We walked the meadows, wrapped in each other's arms, whispering our love delightedly, talking of our hopes and dreams.

As the moon rose, silvering the green velvet of deep Charter's Wood, I stood in the shelter of his arm, his cloak cast about me.

At first, the noise came so gently on the wind that we scarcely heard it. But then it came louder and stronger: music — eerie and strange, high and uncanny. I clung closer to Tam's side. We had time only to gaze at each other in amazement before the music surrounded us.

Then came the riders. Looming out of the evening mists, strangely silent, the calvalcade passed us by.

First came a great company of riders on black horses, the bells of their harness chiming with a deep, soft tone, their faces blank and empty. Then came the brown, their bridle bells adding a higher note to the ghostly music that enthralled us both.

At last they passed, their heads lowered, their clothes strange, as if belonging to another country, or another time. I could not move for my fear, and I could not look away.

Then came the white riders. They were so beautiful that I felt them draw me: I began to go to them — but Tam's arm held me still.

I saw the glitter of jewels on their rich velvet cloaks and the sweep of silken sleeves. And from the harness of their horses, a thousand silver bells added magic to the music that swelled all about us like the sea in caves on distant shores.

In the midst of them all — I saw her. She was lovelier than the rising moon. Raven hair floated in a swirling cloud about her shoulders. She wore a long, flowing gown of velvet of the deepest green, fastened with silver and clasped with shimmering moonstones. From every knot of her horse's mane, and every link of her harness, hung the haunting silver bells.

She dazzled me with her pale beauty. As I felt Tam stiffen, and then his whole body tremble, coldness came into my heart. Slowly, she turned to us, with her eyes of emerald fire. She looked at Tam, standing tall and fair and strong — and she smiled.

The riders passed, the black, the brown and the white. She'd gone, vanished away with the silver music, into the depths of the forest. I wanted only to run. But Tam stood as if turned to stone. I called out his name again and again, frantically pulling at his arms and cloak, to take him away from that terrible place.

AT last, he spoke my name slowly, questioningly. I took his hand and led him back to the village. But the eyes that looked into mine were the eyes of a stranger.

At the farm, his mother and brothers took him in. When I told them of the lady of the forest, their eyes clouded and they wouldn't look at me.

That night I lay awake, tossing in fear and anguish. I rose with the dawn to go to him. But I was too late. He had vanished without trace.

"Where did he go?" I cried. "When? You must know!" His brothers looked guiltily at each other, and said nothing. I turned

to his mother. But she looked at me sadly, with unshed tears in her eyes.

"No," she said. "There's nothing we can do. If she wants him, she'll have him. We cannot fight her."

"The Green Lady? But who is she? What has she done . . . I would fight her, or anyone, for Tam!"

She shook her head. "You can't, Janet," she said sadly. "It was the Queen of the Elfkind you saw. She, and all Her dark court. She's not of this earth. Whatever she wants, she takes. She always has, and always will."

I gazed at her in disbelief. "But . . . but those are just stories," I gasped. "They're not true, I don't believe them!"

But her eyes told me that she believed.

She wouldn't say more and I knew that I alone would search for him. I ran towards the village, heedless of the briars that caught in my skirts and cloak, asking everyone I saw. But when I mentioned the Green Lady, they, too, looked afraid then shook their heads and hurried away.

As I stood at the edge of the village, weary and near to tears, I heard an old, dry voice speak my name. Slowly, I looked up. She was old and bent, but her eyes were bright as a bird's.

I recognised the wise old woman who gathered herbs on the edge of the forest, and made medicines for the villagers. She was beckoning me from her cottage door. As if in a dream, I entered.

"Tell me," she said, and she sat quite still and silent as I told her of the riders in the evening, and Tam's disappearance.

"Do you know who she is?" she asked at last.

"Yes, but . . . I can't believe what they told me . . ."

"Then you must believe," said the old woman.

"But I won't believe in magic, it can't be real . . ."

"What is magic?" she said. "I cannot say whether she has the power of magic or not, and I cannot say

whether she is truly of this earth or of some other, but this I do know: the Queen of the Elfkind is a powerful and dangerous enemy and it goes hard with those who cross her.

SHE'S the Lady of the Woods, leader of the people of the forests and hills. They've always been with us through the ages, led by their Lady gowned in green. People have always feared them."

"Then . . . are they spirits?" I asked, more afraid, almost ready to believe. "Can she truly make magic?"

"They aren't spirits. And whether it is magic or not, I cannot say. But the Elf-Queen and her followers do have the power, and once someone falls under their influence, they become the bound and mindless servants of the Lady until death frees them. Unless . . ."

"Unless?" I asked, my breath coming faster.

"Unless a free mortal has enough courage and love to set them free."

I looked up at her with sudden hope.

"Do you truly love him?" she asked.

I could only nod.

"Is your courage as strong as your love, child? Once she draws you in, you're lost."

"If I can't win Tam back," I said slowly, "I'd rather be lost than live without him."

She looked at me for a long, silent moment, before nodding. "Then you shall try. I'll tell you all I know, but remember only you can do it."

She went on, "At the rise of the full moon, the Elf-Queen leaves the forest to visit her subjects in the far forests of the land, and to seek young men to become her knights. When her eye falls on them, they are powerless to disobey.

"If you would free Tam Linn, you must lie in wait at the next full moon, until the riders leave the forest. Silently, you must wait whilst the black and the

Continued on page 82

# YOU DON'T OWN ME!

*When I finished with Dave, he said he'd make me sorry – but I didn't realise just how far he'd go . . .*

**R**IGHT from the start, I knew Dave was different from the other boys I'd been out with. He was quieter, more serious — that was what attracted me to him in the first place.

But I never dreamed he'd get serious about me! Nobody else ever had — and that was the way I liked it.

I never took things very seriously myself. I reckoned I was too young to be tied down. There was too much fun to be had to even think of going steady yet.

I'd never gone out with one boy for more than a couple of months, but none of them had minded. In fact, I'd stayed friends with most of them even after we'd finished.

But when I tried to explain to Dave how I felt, he just looked at me in amazement.

"But I love you, Liz," he said, in a quiet sort of voice. "I want us to be together for ever."

I thought he was just saying it — I

didn't realise he really meant it — even when he told me he couldn't bear the thought of me going out with anyone else.

I tried to make a joke of it.

"If I find a queue of guys at my door, I'm not going to turn them away!" I told him, laughing . "I like to get to know as many people as possible. After all, I'll only be young once!"

But Dave didn't laugh. Instead, a really strange look came into his eyes and, for a moment, a cold shiver ran through me.

"You'll have to say no to other guys in the future then," he said firmly. "You'll have to tell everyone you're my girl now. You *can't* go out with anyone else — I won't let you . . ."

It was my turn to look amazed then. No-one had ever spoken to me like that before. Suddenly, my laughter had gone and in its place was anger.

"You can't stop me, Dave — you don't own me! I'll go out with whoever I want to — and it certainly won't be you — not any more!"

## "I FELT SO SORRY FOR HIM."

I turned to walk away, thinking that was the end of that. Then, suddenly, he was pounding down the street after me, catching hold of my arm.

"Don't leave me, Liz," he was begging, and the expression on his face had changed completely. "You mean the world to me — I don't know what I'd do without you . . ."

When I saw the desperate pleading in his eyes, I felt so sorry for him that all my anger melted. I caught hold of his hand.

"OK, Dave," I sighed. "But don't ask me to go steady, please. I like you — I like you a lot — but I don't want to get involved. I'm too young to go out with just one boy all the time . . ."

I thought he understood then and that everything would be OK again, but instead it got worse and worse. If I so much as spoke to a boy I knew, Dave would turn on me angrily, demand to know who he was and why I was speaking to him.

"You're *my* girl, remember?" he kept saying.

He kept on and on until I couldn't stand it any longer. If Dave insisted it had to be all or nothing, then my choice was made. Dave and I were finished.

"Look, Dave," I tried to reason with him, "you're smothering me. I can't take any more . . ."

If I'd hit him, he couldn't have looked more hurt.

"It's only because I love you, Liz," he insisted. "I'd be lost without you . . ."

He'd got round me that way once before, but this time I was determined.

"Don't be so silly," I said firmly. "Of course you wouldn't be lost. I'm not the only girl in the world. You'll soon find someone else!"

"But I don't *want* someone else, Liz. I only want you . . ."

I'd heard enough. I was beginning to lose patience. I told him we were finished — I never wanted to see him again. Then I walked away and left him standing there.

When he didn't follow me, I thought he'd seen sense at last and wouldn't bother me again. But I was wrong.

## "THERE WAS SOMETHING IN HIS VOICE THAT FRIGHTENED ME."

When a couple of weeks passed and I didn't hear from him, I thought he'd got the message at last. But don't get me wrong, I didn't mean to hurt him — it was just a case of having to be cruel to be kind. I wasn't going to go through life with Dave trailing after me all the time, like some sort of devoted puppy.

It was then I met Steve and realised how much fun I'd been missing. I knew I wasn't the love of Steve's life — but that suited me fine! I could relax and laugh in Steve's company, in a way I'd never been able to do with Dave.

Everything was great — until the night I came hurtling into the house, still giggling to myself about some silly joke Steve'd made on the way home from the disco.

When the phone rang, I nearly jumped out of my skin! I mean, it isn't often the phone rings at midnight.

I picked up the receiver slowly.

"I saw you tonight, Liz." It was Dave, but there was something in his voice that frightened me. "I saw who you were with. I saw you laughing and having fun . . ."

"So?" I tried to keep calm as his voice tailed off. "I can have fun if I want, can't I? You don't own me !"

"But you own *me*, Liz! You own my heart and you own my soul. I can't go on without you . . ."

I slammed the phone down, but my hands were trembling and I felt sick as Dave's words kept going through my mind.

## "I FELT THE FAMILIAR FEAR RETURN . . ."

Even seeing Steve the next evening didn't really help to take my mind off Dave's threats.

"What's wrong, Liz?" Steve asked finally. "You're really quiet tonight. Has something upset you?"

And, suddenly glad for the chance to get it off my chest, I told him what Dave had said.

"You want to take no notice of him, love," Steve said when I'd finished my story. "He's only jealous."

But I shook my head.

"I thought so, too, at first," I admitted. "But now I'm not so sure. He said I was the only one he wanted — and he said he couldn't go on without me . . ."

My voice shook a bit as I said that and, for a moment, Steve held me tightly, then he told me again to take no notice.

"He's just saying that to make you feel awful," he added. "He doesn't mean it. He'll soon find someone else, forget about you . . ."

I wanted to believe Steve then, I really did, but somehow I couldn't quite forget Dave's words. I couldn't forget the expression on his face that night I finished with him . . .

For the next couple of days, every time the phone rang, I always got Mum or someone to answer, just in case it was him.

Then, on the Friday night, I was in by myself when the phone rang. I'd been getting ready to meet Steve and it was his voice I expected to hear when I picked up the receiver.

When I realised it was Dave again, I felt the familiar fear return . . .

"You've got to go out with me again, Liz," he kept pleading. "Please. Without you, I've nothing . . ."

"Oh, for goodness' sake, Dave —" I started to say to him, but he interrupted.

"Look, Liz," he insisted, "I've got to see you. Please! Meet me at eight outside Jenners' Café ."

"But I'm going out already!" I said as firmly as I could, although inside I'd started to tremble. "Steve's taking me to a concert. The tickets cost a fortune and I've really been looking forward to it. Anyway, I've told you before, it's all over between us. How many times do I have to tell you, Dave?"

"OK — but you'll be sorry for the way you're treating me. You'll wish you'd listened . . ."

He hung on just long enough to make sure his words had sunk in, then hung up before I could reply.

I told Steve about it just as soon as he arrived, but he shook his head.

"Stop upsetting yourself, Liz," he said. "He's just trying to spoil things

Continued on page 78

# YOU DON'T OWN ME!

Continued from page 77

for us. He's mad because you're going out with me instead of him. You hurt his pride when you finished with him, so he's trying to have his revenge . . .

"Try to forget all about him — concentrate on enjoying the concert instead!"

The concert was so good that I did enjoy every minute of it and, by the time I got home, Dave was forgotten.

I made a cup of coffee and sat down to drink it, then suddenly the phone started ringing.

Oh, no, I thought, it can't be . . .

## "I SOMEHOW FELT RESPONSIBLE . . ."

But the voice at the other end wasn't Dave's. It was a woman — but I could hardly make out what she was saying, she sounded so upset.

"Liz, is that you? This is Dave's mum. I-I'm afraid there's been an accident."

I tried to think clearly, but somehow I couldn't bring myself to ask any of the questions that were buzzing round inside my head. Maybe I didn't want to know the answers.

". . . a crash," the voice went on. "He's just regained consciousness and he's asking for you. Please, Liz, will you come to the hospital?"

Dad agreed to drive me there and I tried to sort out my confused thoughts on the way. A crash? But Dave didn't even drive and neither did any of his mates, as far as I knew. Then what . . .?

When we arrived, Dave's parents were waiting for us, anxious and white-faced.

"I'm sorry, Liz," his mum stepped forward. "I know you're not going out with Dave any more — but he keeps asking for you . . ."

But before I saw Dave, I had to know what'd happened. I somehow felt responsible for all this, although I knew Steve would've told me I was being stupid.

Dave's mum and dad exchanged a look I couldn't fathom, then his dad said quietly, "Dave took our car from the drive, Liz. He'd had a row with his mum, you see. She'd heard him

phoning you and told him to leave you alone." His voice tailed off, then he added, "It's not the first time this sort of thing's happened . . ."

"Not the first time?" I echoed blankly. Nothing seemed to make sense any more.

"Dave's always been a bit, well, oversensitive, Liz," his mum explained gently. "There was another girl, a couple of years ago. When she finished with him, he really made her life a misery. He even ran away from home for a time when she refused to have anything more to do with him . . ."

Between sobs, his mum went on to tell me how Dave had driven their car recklessly from the house before they could stop him. He said he was on his way over to my house — that he had to stop me before I went out with Steve. But he never got there.

Halfway across town, he'd seen a police car, and panicked. He lost control of the car, and it swerved and crashed into a parked car.

"The doctors say he'll be OK, Liz, but we've been told he'll probably need psychiatric treatment. But whatever Dave says to you, Liz, don't let him try to make you feel guilty in any way." She patted my arm reassuringly. "Will you go in and see him now?"

It wasn't easy talking to Dave after what'd happened. Even seeing him lying there in that hospital bed, I could hardly bring myself to feel sorry for him, knowing all the heartache he'd caused.

He did tell me he was sorry about everything and that he'd leave me alone in future, but whether he'd have kept that promise, I'll never know, for as soon as he was discharged from hospital, his parents moved away and he went with them.

I suppose it'll be a long time before Dave gets over all this, but I hope one day he'll realise that you can't force people to fall in love, no matter how desperately you want them to. I hope he realises, not just for his own sake, but because I'd hate any other girl to go through the same ordeal I've suffered.

---

EVER wondered how your boy will turn out once the first flush of his love for you has faded? Will he be mad, bad or just plain boring? No use asking his mates — take a sneaky peek at his home life instead. His family have all the facts!

## MUM'S THE WORD

So he takes you home for Sunday tea, and there it is all spread out on the table. Three-cornered watercress sarnies, juicy slabs of fruitcake, the best china — a spread fit for a queen. No, it's not you. Here she comes, the queen of 43 Acacia Avenue (pause for fanfares) . . . his mum!

She's lovely, she's immaculate in her nice hairdo and smart dress. You turn into a quivering jelly 'cos you know you can't compete with Wonder Mum!

But don't panic. Peep under the sideboard when she's not looking. See that dust? Lift up a corner of the carpet. Spot the crumbs swept neatly underneath? Celebrate with another slice of her absolutely delicious . . . *home-baked* . . . cake?

"Of course, dear! An old recipe handed down from my great-granny . . ."

Try not to stare at the cake box that says, "Bunn The Baker" — the box she forgot to hide away! She's human, after all!

Always make friends with his mum. Not only will she give him back-handers from the housekeeping to take you out, she will be the World's Greatest Authority on your boy.

Offer to help her with the washing-up and by the time you get to the coffee cups you will have discovered all about his in-growing toenail, his bad moods, his passion for bedsocks and how he still plays with toy boats in the bath. Now you will be able to decide whether he is really such a bargain boy after all . . . !

## JUST LIKE HIS DAD . . .

Remember, though, that his mum is biased. She loves her little soldier, after all. These are only his *good* points she has revealed to you.

If you want to see whether he's *really* got a nasty side, you needn't look further than his

# ASK THE FAMILY!

dad. If you can find him. Try the potting shed, under the family car, up in the attic, and the compost heap.

If he is (a) tending to his prize marrows, (b) cooing to the pet pigeons, or (c) brewing home-made wine, you are on to a good thing, here.

Your boy will turn out to be just like Dad in the long run. (Due to many years of delicious home-grown vegetables, home-brewed plonk and being lulled to sleep by dove-like sounds from the attic.)

If, however, Dad is down the pub, watching football or taking six engines to bits on the kitchen floor — beware! If Wonder Mum can't make her hubby behave, what chance do you stand with their son?

But should Dad turn out to be a lovable sort, whatever his hobbies, hang on in there! Because a dad who likes you will make sure that son of his always treats you right!

## HAVING A GRAN' OLD TIME

Pay special attention to the way your guy treats his granny. Does he fetch her slippers, feed her fruit cake, never moan when it's mince again for tea because Gran can't get her falsers round a bit of roast beef?

Aaaaah! Ain't he sweet? Either that or she's promised to

## Mum's the word when it comes to

## getting the low-down on

## your favourite fella!

leave him Grandpa's priceless collection of antique soldering irons in her will . . .

## STAY CLEAR OF KID SISTER

There's not much point in getting an opinion from his little sis. She hates him anyway. In fact, she thinks all boys are stupid. But she'll love you.

Within seconds, she'll have emptied your handbag on the floor, dragged out all your make-up and hauled you off to play with her dollies.

Let's face it, you don't

really need her revelations about your boy, do you? And you definitely don't need your fave lipstick all over your best dress, three splodged-up mascaras and purple eye-shadow ground into her mum's (new) lounge carpet . . .

## BROTHERLY LOVE

If he's got a big brother who's out on the town every night, is the neighbourhood heart-throb, rides a motor-bike that Eddie Kidd would drool over and earns a fortune — beware! Your boy

will stop at nothing to follow in Big Brother's footsteps!

This could mean you'll be left at home night after night, get

premature wrinkles from worry about slippery roads and whether he's got his crash helmet on right — and be broke. (All his wages will go on the bike and nights out with the boys.)

It's no use trying to change him. He'll have his brother's image to live up to. So do yourself a favour — settle for Big Brother instead — he'll soon have had his fill of wild living and want to settle down to a nice normal life!!

## PETS' CORNER!

If his family have no pets and Dad jokes that they don't need any, 'cos your boy is all the beast their household can cope with, ho, ho, ho . . . This is Bad News. He may have a warped sense of humour. On the other hand, he surely knows what he's talking about . . .

But chances are, there's a moth-eaten old Puss or Rover tucked away somewhere. (Take care about what you wipe your feet on!) And if your fella dotes on this pet, you've landed yourself a winner.

Watch him as he strokes Tiddles, cuddles Fang, lets Billy-Boy nibble his ear and tells him what a pretty boy he is. If he gives you half as much affection, he's worth hanging on to!

Continued on page 84   81

## The Magic Of Love...

Continued from page 75

brown riders pass, for they are Elf-Lords, and can never be freed.

"But then will come the white riders, and among them the Lady. They're earthly men who've fallen under her spell, and Tam will ride among them. You must run swiftly to him, catch hold of his bridle, pull him down and hold him fast.

"Then, whatever may happen, you must hold him close. Think only of your love, and close your mind to the things which will appear to you."

Her words echoed in my mind in the seemingly endless days that followed. I thought often of the Dark Lady of the Woods, but my mind shied away from the thought of what might happen when I came, at last, face to face with the power of the Elfkind.

That night, the full moonlight fell as cold as death on field and tree. I stood alone at the edge of the forest. Tight bands of fear pressed about my throat. I whispered Tam's name and tried to imagine him standing before me in the moonlight, to see his eyes before the laughter froze out of them. But I couldn't.

When the tinkling music began on the silver air, I started pulling my cloak around me, to stop the shaking of my hands.

I didn't have long to wait. Their harnesses ringing, the company of black riders emerged from the forest, and passed me by. Then came the brown riders, silent, save for the unearthly music of their silver bells, so close I could have reached out and touched them.

And then, the white. She rode in the midst of them all, shining in her loveliness, gowned in the green of the forests. My heart almost failed me, for I sensed her power, as old as time itself.

But by her side rode Tam. He, too, wore green, with silver bells on his harness, and a star on his breast. His eyes were fixed on the Lady, empty, aware of nothing but her.

LOVE and despair urged me forward. I threw myself among the horses and seized the bridle of Tam's great, white horse. As the reins fell from his fingers, I caught his hands, and pulling him down from the saddle, wrapped my shaking arms about his cold and rigid body.

I heard a furious cry go up from the Elf-Riders. Their horses whirled, and bore down on me: their nostrils breathing fire and their hooves flaying out as if to crush me.

And as I stood, weakened with terror, I held in my arms not Tam, but a vast scaled serpent. I cried out, and almost — almost released it. But in time I remembered.

I forced myself to believe that I truly held Tam. As I clung to the writhing coils, I heard the shrill, harsh voice of the Elf-Queen — not silvery, not beautiful, but raucous and ugly —

"What do you seek in our realm, weak daughter of Eve?"

And I replied as steadily as I could, "I seek my own, Tam Linn, and I hold him."

The scaled serpent twisted once more in my arms, but I held it tight. The threatening faces of the riders and their fiery horses still surrounded me.

Suddenly the air was filled with fire and smoke. Choking and half-blinded by tears, I clung to the mass of searing flame, which crackled through the tangle of thorns I held. I heard the harsh Elf-voice once more, but still I replied that I held Tam Linn.

As if in a nightmare, I held in my arms a slimy toad, an eagle that battered mighty wings to be free, a great black dog with burning eyes — but still I clung on, for somewhere in my dazed and fading mind I knew that I still held Tam.

My voice now only a whisper, I said, "I seek my own, Tam Linn, and I hold him." And then I knew that, truly, I did hold him. The body I knew was lying heavily in my aching, clinging arms. Summoning up the last of my strength, I flung my cloak about him, as the Wise Woman had said, and cried out, "Tam Linn is free!"

A wild shriek of fury went up from the Elfkind as their power was broken. As I sank in exhaustion, clinging to Tam, the riders — the black, the brown and the white — whirled about us and vanished into the moonlit forest.

At last I raised my head from his shoulder, and Tam's eyes opened. For an instant he gazed at me blankly. Then his eyes cleared and he knew me. Love dawned there again, and I wept with joy.

He held me close, drawing my head down again on to his shoulder. And for a long time I was aware only of the beating of his heart, and the scent of falling honeysuckle.

**The End.**

PARTIES are great places to find blokes, right? If you don't manage to corner them in the kitchen you can always lock 'em in the loo or even squeeze together with six of the best in a broom cupboard and pretend you're playing "Sardines"!

There's just one tiny problem, though, which we aim to help you solve. And that is . . .

. . . how do you sort out the nice guys from the nasties?

### Gasp! It's The Gatecrashers!

This sort never comes alone. There's always a great gang of them, all leaning on each other for support. Take care one doesn't trap you against a wall and lean on *you*! He'll bend your ears with lines like . . .

"Where've you been hiding all my — hic! — life, babe? Fanshy a danshe, eh? C'mon, that'sh what we're here for, to have a good time, right? Like your dressh, green really suits you — matches your eyes. Hey, lads, look at this tasty little mover I've landed! Wot? Oh, it's a rubber plant. Shilly me!"

There's only one thing to do if a gruesome gatecrasher comes near you — gatecrash yourself . . . out of the party.

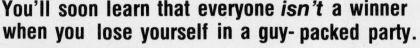

# Party Prize Guys!

**You'll soon learn that everyone *isn't* a winner when you lose yourself in a guy-packed party.**

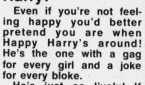

## Gosh! It's Nosher!

Now it's time to meet Nigel the Nosher! You'll meet him in the kitchen — definitely! While you're quietly trying to decide between a twiglet and a tuna sarnie the door will burst open and you'll be knocked to one side as Nigel lunges for the table.

You'll recognise Nigel by his resemblance to the Incredible Hulk — he's large but he's not green — yet. Just wait until he's demolished the buffet!

His eyes will flash round the room until they come to rest on the object of his desires. No, not you — the mountain of sausage rolls behind you! You'd better get out of the way fast before he mistakes you for a turkey!

Before you can say, "Sixty-eight cheese sarnies with the crusts cut off" he'll be in there, demolishing grub like he hasn't seen food for a fortnight.

He's amazing, he even manages to chat you up between mouthfuls.

"Pass me that plate, will you, darlin'? Mmmm, tasty. Just my type — with pickle. I love that bit of — munch — sauce. You're — chew, slurp — kinda saucy yourself, doll! Gobble, gobble, gulp. Second helpings? Ooh, ta!"

Take some advice. When he dives head first into the fridge — and he *will* when he hears there's cheesecake in there — do him and everyone else a favour. Shove him in and shut the door . . .

## Bert The Bore . . . Yawn, Zzzzzz

It isn't just girls who turn into wallflowers at parties, you know. Take this weed, for instance!

Bert is the one who props up the corner of the room all evening desperately trying to look cool and aloof. Shame! He looks about as mysterious as a soggy crisp! DON'T feel sorry for this wimp, though, whatever you do, because he really is boring.

He doesn't actually like parties, you see. Mostly he wonders why on earth he bothered to drag himself along to such a dump. But he doesn't often wonder because that would mean using his brain and that's so — ho-hum, yawn — exhausting.

He just knew this party would be awful — so it is. Best thing you can do for this boy is to leave him muttering to himself in the corner. After all, the only company he's looking for is his own — it can't answer back!

## Swoon! It's Lennie The Leerer!

Tall, dark and you'll havesome, this guy's a real dazzler. If only you could get your hands on him. No chance! He's far too busy chatting up that blonde in the body stocking . . . and the dizzy redhead in the glitter mini . . . and the brunette in the plunge neckline . . . and he's not wasting *any* time.

He disappears at regular intervals. If you're desperate you can track him down, though. He'll be wrapped round a female in some dark corner.

Lennie really loves parties, preferably with wall-to-wall girls. And rest assured, he'll get to know them all before the night's out.

So, you *really* want a five-minute flutter with this Casanova? Well, that's all you'll get before his eyes alight on someone new — and he'll be off in her direction, lips a-quiver!

## Ha-ha-ha-happy Harry!

Even if you're not feeling happy you'd better pretend you are when Happy Harry's around! He's the one with a gag for every girl and a joke for every bloke.

He's just so lively! If he's not dancing on the table, he'll be standing on his head and drinking punch. Then he'll leap up and slap you on the back before blowing up a balloon and bursting it in your ear. For Harry, parties have got to be fun, fun, FUN!

Trouble is, Harry wants everyone else to have fun, too. And that includes you over in the corner. If he catches you doing nothing, he'll drag you on to the floor and soon you'll be tangoing and waving your undies in the air!

Worst thing is, you've no option! So, if Harry spots *you* give a cheery grin, blow on your party hooter and tell him the one about the chimpanzee and the vicar. That should keep him happy and it's better than doing the tango!

## Prize Guys

Once you've eliminated the rubbish you can get down to the serious business of finding yourself a decent boy. Wherever they are.

And hey, where *are* they? Surely, they can't all have gone home, *yet*? Better check out the kitchen, the coal bunker — everywhere.

When you spot one, don't waste any time — grab him and make a run for it. There's nothing like a nice romantic stroll for getting acquainted, and for getting you home safe and sound.

Then, if he asks you for a date, agree by all means — as long as he doesn't take you to a party!

Continued from page 81

THE END

85

# The sky's the limit!

*at least it is for air hostesses! Our special careers feature reveals all about the girls who have their heads in the clouds.*

WHO'D want to be an air hostess? OK, OK, hands down, the lot of you! Judging by the number of letters sent in to our problem page each week, quite a few of you would like to be high flyers!

We went along to Gatwick Airport to investigate the facts behind the girls with their heads in the clouds! Our hosts (or hostesses!) for the day were the staff of British Caledonian, one of Britain's leading airlines. Caroline, who's been with the company for just over a year now, showed us the ropes.

## SELECTION TIME

"British Caledonian receive over 20,000 applications each year from would-be hostesses," Caroline told us, "and of these only 120-150 will be successful.

"Most of these enquiries are from girls who're far too young to be air hostesses — the minimum age's twenty."

Here's some of the other qualifications you'll need . . .

EDUCATION — You must've had a good standard of education, and preference is given to applicants who've attained O-level standard.

SWIMMING — You must be able to swim at least 25 yards.

LANGUAGES — It's an advantage to be able to speak one or more foreign language.

HEIGHT — 5 ft. 4 in.-5 ft. 10 in. (160 cm-175 cm).

"The airlines don't have anything against small girls," Caroline said, laughing. "It's just that all airport equipment is standardised, and you have to be a certain height to reach it!"

FIRST AID — Although some training is given, it's desirable to have a basic knowledge of First Aid — and a current certificate is even better.

"In addition to these, there are also certain requirements about nationality, appearance and personality."

## TRAINING

"All air hostesses undergo a five-week training course, followed by five months, on-the-job training," Caroline went on to say. "After this you're fully qualified as a Junior Cabin Attendant — the proper name for air hostesses. It certainly doesn't sound quite so glamorous, though, does it?

"Here's a run-down of the training course I was on . . .

## WEEK ONE

"After having photos taken for our security passes, we were taken to the training school. There we were introduced to our new company — and learnt about its history and aims for the future.

"After that we were issued with our uniforms — unlike most airlines, British Caledonian offer a choice of nine different tartans.

"Male cabin staff (who're outnumbered by us girls by six to one!) wear dark blue trousers, a tartan jacket and a peaked cap.

"Over the next few days, we learned about aviation terminology, first aid, emergency childbirth and aviation security.

"Next we were advised about make-up — it's vital that you still look good, even at the end of a long and tiring flight. Prolonged flying in pressurised aircraft causes dry skin problems, but we were given expert tuition to help us combat this.

"We were offered a choice of Boots 17 and Christian Dior make-up — and we had discussions as to which cosmetics would go with which tartan."

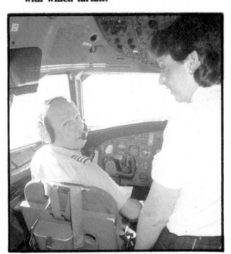

Caroline has a quick word with the captain.

Let's make-up!

## WEEKS TWO AND THREE

Caroline told us that the safety and survival aspect was the most important part of all training — by law, airlines must carry stewards and stewardesses who would be able to cope in any emergency.

"We were all issued with a manual," Caroline continued, "which gave details of all emergency equipment and procedures for the four types of aircraft British Caledonian use.

"The first few days of survival training were taken up with the different types of emergencies which could arise during a flight.

"Instruction was given in the use of anti-smoke oxygen equipment, fire fighting, distress rockets and flares — and it was all backed up with practical

Caroline fetches a fizzy drink for a passenger.

demonstrations.

"British Caledonian even have two old planes which're used as smoke chambers. It was quite scary — but at least we learned what we'd have to do if faced with a real emergency!"

## PRETTY AS A DITCH-ER!

Another important part of safety and survival training is the "wet ditching", when the girls are given a chance to show off their water skills!

"Firstly, we were shown how to use baby survival cots — and then we did life-jacket drill. After that, it was time to man the lifeboat! As you can see from the photographs, it starts off life pretty small — but when it's fully inflated, it's capable of holding up to 60 people!

"We were all shown how to rescue passengers from the water, and bring them into the lifeboat. It was great fun — but at the same time, we *did* see how necessary it was to stay calm in an emergency."

## WEEKS FOUR AND FIVE

The last two weeks of the course are given over to cabin services training. Caroline explained why.

"Passengers base their opinion of an airline mainly on the service and attention they receive during their flight. So we try to make their trip as enjoyable as we can, and hope we help them get their holiday or business trip off to the best possible start!

"We actually start work long before the passengers even board the plane," Caroline says, smiling. "We have to check that everything is in the right place, and that all the safety equipment is stored away.

"And although many of the lessons were taught in a classroom we spent a lot of time in a mock-up section of an aircraft cabin.

"It came complete with the galley, which is the name for the little kitchen area you get on planes. It was good fun — we took turns at serving meals to each other!

"Most in-flight meals are pre-packed — chefs and kitchen staff work at Gatwick Airport preparing and packing food. All we have to do is heat up the meals!

"Sometimes, though, we have passengers with special requirements, perhaps because of medical or religious reasons. And we have to be prepared for babies, too — an eighteen-month-old toddler is going to find it a bit difficult eating roast beef and potatoes!

"We also occasionally have passengers who require special attention, for one reason or another. Expectant mothers, invalids, unaccompanied children, all need to be looked after — and you have to be sympathetic to their problems."

At the end of their training, all the students complete a three-part examination, and if they're successful in this, they graduate as Junior Cabin Attendants.

At a special celebration lunch, each student is individually presented with her "wings and aircrew licence".

"It's a great moment," Caroline says. "It made all the hours of training worthwhile. And even though that was almost a year ago — and I've flown thousands of miles since — I've enjoyed every minute of it all!"

*FURTHER INFORMATION: Application forms and further information about British Caledonian can be obtained from Cabin Staff Recruitment, British Caledonian Airways, Cabin Services Department, London Airport-Gatwick, Horley, Surrey.*

*Although this feature is about British Caledonian Airways, other airlines have similar training schemes. Check with your local reference library for addresses of other airlines you may be interested in.*

It's in the bag!

You push, and I'll pull!

One-two-three — heave!     Legs and Co!     How many more can we fit in, then?

# The Perfect Wedding Dress

OK—MAYBE A DRESS SHOP'S NOT THE MOST ROMANTIC PLACE IN THE WORLD . . .

. . . BUT I BET I HEAR MORE ROMANTIC STORIES IN ONE WEEK THAN YOU READ IN A DOZEN MAGAZINES! TAKE THAT GIRL, LAURA, YESTERDAY . . .

I- I'D LIKE TO LOOK AT THE WEDDING DRESSES, PLEASE.

CERTAINLY—WE'VE GOT SOME BEAUTIFUL ONES IN JUST NOW.

Bridal

Continued on page 92

# Add A Touch Of
# Seasoning!

Blue Jeans Beauty

**If you want to look great all year round, you've got to plan your beauty routine, month by month. So, here's our special Blue Jeans guide on what to do when, to help you be a four-seasons stunner!**

## JANUARY

OK, it's cold outside and you're covered in a thick layer of woollies, BUT start the New Year with a firm resolution to . . . GET YOUR FIGURE IN TRIM!

If you really can't face the thought of outdoor exercise (coward!) then do try some indoor exercises, like . . . cycling in the air (for hips), knee bends and stretching (for thighs), and arms raised, legs straight, feet apart and touch your toes (for waist and midriff bulges).

Try swimming once or twice each week and make a point of walking at least part of the way to work or school.

DON'T huddle in front of the fire or radiator 'cos it's bad for the circulation (yes, chilblains!!) and equally bad for the complexion too, as artificial heat tends to dry up all the skin's natural oils!

## FEBRUARY

Now's the time to take a good look at your poor, suffering skin! Not just on your face — but all over! Moisturiser is a MUST when the air outside is cold and drying and the air inside is warm and drying!

Any money you have to spend this month should go on baby lotion or any other all-over moisture cream and a good lip salve to help prevent dry, cracked lips.

Take a look at what you're eating and don't fall into the trap of thinking you need lots of stodgy puds and cake to fill you up 'cos it's cold. Fresh or stewed fruit is just as good as treacle tart, and two green veg. will do more for your figure and complexion than double chips!

## MARCH

Winds really play havoc with hair, so just as last month we put moisture back into our skins, this month we should think about protecting our hair.

Forget about expensive shop-bought conditioners and try a coconut oil treatment instead. (It's suitable for all hair types and can be bought in a jar from a chemist at about 40p!)

Warm the jar in hot (not boiling!) water, and when the contents turn oily pour a little into the palm of your hand and rub it into the hair ends and then your scalp. Keep a warm towel wrapped round your head for about an hour afterwards, then shampoo in the usual way.

A jar lasts ages, so do this about every third or fourth shampoo and you'll soon feel your hair softer and silkier!

## APRIL

Look on the bright side — sunshine might be just around the corner . . . so you'd better get your body ready for stripping off (well, a layer or two, anyway!). Your skin'll be soft from the moisturising you've been giving it — BUT it might be dull, dingy and a bit pimply from being covered up through the winter months.

A loofah is the answer. When you're in the bath, rub it gently on hard and lumpy skin areas like the tops of legs and arms, bottom and heels.

DON'T go mad and scrub away until your skin is red raw! Little and often each bath time is ideal . . . to get your circulation going and your skin glowing!

P.S. Make an appointment to see the dentist for your first check up this year.

## MAY

Time to think about your hands and feet, elbows and knees. Invest in some hand cream and rub it lavishly into your hands and feet each evening after washing.

Always use an emery board to shape your nails, and if you want to wear nail polish make sure you've got remover on hand . . . 'cos nothing looks worse than chipped painted nails. Ugh!

Try on last year's swimming costume or bikini and anything else you just might be bulging out of! Take note of any bulges in the wrong places and resolve to carry on faithfully with your exercise routine — or take it up again if you'd stopped!

## JUNE

Check up on suntan lotions and oils and summery make-up. Sun protection creams are generally better than oils for most skins and for convenience (they don't cause as much damage if they leak!). Don't think you necessarily get better results through buying an expensive brand 'cos it just isn't always true. The art of successful tanning is to put the cream on OVER a layer of ordinary moisturiser so it glides on better and works more efficiently!

If you've been in the habit of using dark make-up, like brown and dark greens on your eyes and deep plummy colours on your lips, now's the time to turn to softer

## SEPTEMBER

If you've managed to get a tan and want to hang on to it just that little bit longer . . . two tips for you. First, keep on with the all-over body moisturising, and second, eat plenty of citrus fruit like oranges, grapefruit, tangerines and blackcurrants, 'cos the Vitamin C in them actually helps you keep your tan longer.

Don't throw away empty halves of lemon peel — use them on dry hands and elbows. Simply pour a little olive or almond oil into the halves and let your elbows soak in them. After a few minutes, pour the lemony, oily liquid on to your hands. Rub in thoroughly, then smooth what's left on to your knees and heels.

## OCTOBER

All that sun and dry wind means your hair'll need a little extra attention now. Are your ends looking straggly and uneven? Get them trimmed off! Both skin and hair could benefit from conditioning treatments this month, so keep three evenings aside to pamper face and hair.

Try a face mask of a tub of natural yogurt mixed with a tablespoonful of clear honey. Leave it on for ten minutes, then rinse off with warm water. For hair, get back to the coconut oil treatment, or try an egg yolk rubbed into the hair ends AFTER shampooing . . . rinse off in lukewarm water. Don't waste the white if you have a normal or oily skin, but whip it up till it's frothy then apply to your face as a mask. It's super for absorbing grease and leaving skin glowing.

## NOVEMBER

Before you start ear-marking money for Christmas pressies, make sure you've enough eye make-up remover (or baby oil) and nail polish remover to last you through the party season. 'Cos chances are if you don't buy it now you won't have the cash to spare later.

If you can afford to treat yourself, how about a bottle of perfume to make you feel feminine and mysterious (even if you haven't anything new to wear!) when those party invitations come in?

On cold evenings spent indoors try experimenting with make-up — don't leave it until "the night" before trying something new . . . it might not work!! Get a pal or two round and swap cosmetics.

Fix the second of your twice-yearly dental appointments.

## DECEMBER

Christmas is nearly here and it's time to sparkle. So you're only going carol-singing with the gang — what's to stop you sparkling anyway!

Always wear a little moisturiser all day, every day, to protect your skin, and make a point of drinking at least three glasses of clear, cold, tap water each day, 'cos it really does help keep your body ticking over nicely and stops you looking all grey and wintry!

Check that your party glad-rags are all ready to wear with jammed zips, stains, missing buttons, split seams all taken care of.

Whatever size or shape you are, think carefully about what you eat for the first three weeks of the month to allow you to go a little mad for the last week or so. Make an effort to cut out fattening, spot-making foods like cakes, pastries, biscuits and sweets, fried foods and more than the occasional portion of chips — not only for your figure's sake, but for your complexion too.

Don't go hungry, just keep tucking in to super big helpings of winter green vegetables, fruit, cheese (especially cottage and Edam) natural yoghurt, eggs, wholemeal bread, crispbread, and plainly-cooked fish, meat and chicken. You can add a touch of seasoning to them to make them tastier!

shades of aquamarine greens, soft blues and lipsticks in more transparent and shimmery shades of clear pink or peach.

The stronger light of summer makes dark colours look too harsh — so you have to be more subtle.

## JULY

Look and feel healthy and summery by trying to get a better tan. If all you get are a few freckles, don't complain — as a light, sunkissed look is often more flattering on pale, British skins than a solid brown. To make pale legs glisten and look more attractive, rub in a moisturiser each morning before you go out.

If you're wearing sandals, be extra careful about foot hygiene (that means a cool-to-warm wash, morning and evening!). July bathtimes call for a little extra pampering, too, so add a capful of baby oil to your bathwater to soften skin and make it ready for the sun.

If you hair is long, try wearing it up, perhaps in a topknot or plaits (see pages 65-67 for some great styles!) as off-the-neck hair-dos look terrific with T-shirts or strappy sundresses.

## AUGUST

Maybe you aren't wearing any make-up just now, BUT you still need to be careful about cleansing every night. At this time of year, damp faces plus hot dusty atmospheres mean dirtier faces!

Make a special point of cleansing thoroughly round the nose, forehead and chin area, where blackheads and spots are most common.

Use a creamy cleanser on dryish skins, a milk cleanser on normal to oily skins and a mild soap on very oily skins (or you can cleanse, then finish with a soap and water wash!). ALWAYS put a thin film of moisturiser on afterwards, whatever your skin type.

If you're holidaying, sunbathing and generally lazing around in the sun, DO put on protective cream BEFORE you expose yourself, and DON'T sit around in one place in one position for hours on end. That's simply asking for a burnt, sore and unattractive skin. Keep moving and tan gradually — starting with just fifteen minutes at first.

Continued from page 89

93